This Mystery Is Great

Husbands, Wives, and the Bride of Christ

By Hal Hammons

Scripture taken from the NEW AMERICAN STANDARD BIBLE, copyright
1960, 1962, 1963, 1968, 1971, 1972, 1973, 1975, 1977, 1995 by The
Lockman Foundation. Used by permission.

Published by:
One Stone Press
979 Lovers Lane
Bowling Green, KY 42103

Printed in the United States of America

ISBN 10: 1-94142-213-6
ISBN 13: 978-1-941422-13-7

ONE STONE
BIBLICAL RESOURCES

Table of Contents

For Taylor and Kylie
May you learn these lessons quicker and easier than I did, and cause less stress for your spouses in so doing than I did.

Foreword

I hate marriage counseling. You see people at their worst. People who you love. People you thought were better than this. People who appear to be on the verge of destroying the most important asset they have in their war against the devil—and perhaps lose that war in the process.

I also love marriage counseling. You have a chance to remind people of the things about marriage that they already know, because (if they are Christians) they read the same textbook you read. You have a chance to provide help that will immeasurably impact their lives on earth for as long as they may live, and in doing so fortify their chances for spending an eternity together in heaven.

People will inspire. People will disappoint. Good news comes. Bad news comes. Stories, hugs, tears and confessions are shared. It is a mixed bag. In the end, it is an opportunity to show what a godly marriage is doing for me, for my wife and daughters, indeed for every aspect of my life.

In fact, it is very much like being a member of the body of Christ.

As Christians, we struggle in our spiritual marriage to the Lord. Often we disappoint. Occasionally, we are unfaithful. Sometimes the marriage does not survive. But thankfully, we have an advantage: we know the "husband" in this relationship will absolutely do His part. There is no failing on His end. The temptation to fix the problems on the other side of the table is alleviated, since there are no such problems. All that is left is to work on ourselves. If we can bring ourselves to do this, we (with the considerable help of Jesus) are guaranteed to have a happy and successful spiritual marriage.

The purpose behind this book is to help both marriages. The relationship between God and His people is repeatedly couched in the figure of marriage—from the jealousy of God in the wilderness to the gut-wrenching saga of Hosea and Gomer to the wedding ceremony in John's Revelation. Paul tells us in no uncertain terms in Ephesians 5:32 that his instruction regarding proper husband-wife relations was actually a lesson about how Christ and His church are to inter-act with and for each other. By examining the relationship in front of our noses, we are given spiritual insight into the more ephemeral relationship between the Lord and His people. By growing in the one, we supply ourselves with the tools and the experience we need to grow in the other.

For the sake of those whom I have counseled, officially and unofficially, over the years, let me emphasize the characters you will meet in this book are fictitious. No connection between them and actual people, either known to me or unknown, should be inferred. All similarities between them and actual individuals and/or couples is coincidental.

I hope and pray this book can provide healing to those who are in pain, perseverance to those who are doing well, and instruction for those who have not yet entered into either or both of the greatest blessings available on earth to humankind.

Love God, and love each other.

Hal Hammons
Pace, Florida
June 2015

Introduction

Let me introduce you to Peter and his wife, Wendy. Peter is a gospel preacher. You do not know either of them. They are fictitious. Let me repeat. They are fictitious. I gave Peter his name because the apostle Peter is, I believe, the only gospel preacher specifically mentioned as having a wife who partnered with him in the work (1 Corinthians 9:5). Peter is certainly not a code name for Hal Hammons, nor Wendy for Tracie Hammons. I cannot stress this point strongly enough.

However, in a sense, you do know Peter and Wendy. Peter is every preacher you have ever known, including me—most of them probably married to a woman like Wendy. We hear stories. We filter gossip. We hug necks. We say prayers. On rare occasions, when asked, we even offer advice. And, there probably is no subject that comes up more consistently, and in a greater variety of forms and with more intensity of emotion, than these two: marriage and the church.

In this book, Peter and Wendy respond to certain situations that come up with regard both to marriage and to church issues. I encourage you to come to your own conclusions. Supply your own answers if none of the ones provided suit you. Peter and Wendy are not "right." Only God has the right answers. But, to my way of thinking, Peter and Wendy are on the right track. I will offer some explanation as to why I think so. You may disagree, and I'm OK with that. As we strive to be His people, we will inevitably differ on precisely how to apply His answers to particular situations that arise. But if we allow ourselves to be directed by the word, motivated by love, and fueled by prayer, we won't go too far wrong. My hope and prayer here is that Peter and Wendy have provided that example.

Books like this are a problem for writers who want to keep their friends. The book needs to be relevant, or else what's the point? On the other hand, it shouldn't be too relevant, if you take my meaning. No matter how many times the writer emphasizes that the characters are fictitious (and they are in this book, I assure you), the reader is bound to see himself or herself in the story somehow, warts exposed to the world. My brethren, especially the fine folks with whom I have fellowship now, should be assured that I am not singling anyone out. I would not embarrass anyone in print for all the world. Seeing yourself in one or more stories simply means (1) you are taking the study seriously, and (2) your problems are not as unique as you might think. Don't take offense; take instruction.

It is no coincidence that the two most important relationships in our lives here on earth—our connection to our spouses and to our brethren—are so controversial and divisive. We feel deeply. Emotions often cloud our judgment. The answers that seem so obvious in dispassionate Bible class sessions can seem far more murky when we are the ones in Satan's crosshairs. This is why we must be so adept at making hypothetical decisions—because they will not remain hypothetical. And if we have rehearsed doing and saying the right thing enough times, we will be in better position to do so when it really counts—whether it is in service to a friend who is struggling, or whether it is we ourselves who are struggling.

Lesson 1

Putting First Things First

Building Godly Marriages Through Godly Values

Regarding his own work and the work of other gospel preachers, Paul writes, "For no man can lay a foundation other than the one which is laid, which is Jesus Christ," (1 Corinthians 3:11). The gospel of Jesus is the underpinnings of every aspect of a Christian's life. This is true whether one marries or not. Many Christians build a considerable part of their lives somewhere else—on material success, on titillation, on popularity, etc. As much as they may claim to have given their lives to the Lord, most of their actual hours and days are reserved for themselves.

Since most decisions made by such Christians are intended to feed the flesh and not the spirit, it is reasonable to expect their decisions regarding courtship and marriage will follow along the same lines. What's more, since commonality is always valued in a potential spouse, it is highly likely that one materialistic Christian will marry another one. This couple is not building their marriage on Jesus; Jesus is an afterthought at best.

An individual Christian may grow out of his or her fleshly appetites and learn to feed the spirit. If he or she is married, the process becomes more difficult. It is tough enough to climb out of a materialistic quagmire. It becomes far more difficult when the love of your life is pulling you back.

Clearly the lesson for the unmarried is, choose someone who will help you get to heaven instead of hindering you. For the one whose already made choice seems to be presenting more challenges to the life of faith than assistance, the lesson will be much harder. One way or another, we must find the strength to turn our lives toward the Lord—even if it is without the help of our "partner."

A Story From The Office

Spencer's dad told him dropping out of college and getting his real estate license would be a big mistake. Never was a son more happy to prove his father wrong. He proved to be a natural, quickly building one of the most successful real estate firms in the area. By the time he was 28, he had sold the business to a national chain, keeping his office there, and had started another business flipping foreclosed homes. He

Spencer and Diane
- Ages: He's 30, she's 28
- Married: 5 years
- Occupations: He's a realtor, she's studying for her real estate license
- Children: 6-month-old girls, Lea and Mia
Problem: Worldliness

was a multi-millionaire. Diane, a steady reader of *Southern Living* and *Town and Country* since she was 12, was doing all the design consulting for Spencer's flips and studying for her own real estate license. Whatever minimal time they were not working was spent to the fullest. A week in Bali. Touching 49 states in their custom motorcycles over one summer. And, of course, designing and redesigning their 5,000 square foot home in the country.

It all changed practically overnight. The real estate market turned. Spencer was forced to settle an expensive lawsuit out of court. Diane announced she was pregnant—with twins.

Their commitment to the church had never been all that steady ("Too many irons in the fire right now," Spencer would always say), although their contribution checks had always been regular and generous. Now it seemed their circumstances were pushing them even further away from their brethren—and, more importantly, from the Lord.

Spencer, naturally, was all over Peter and Wendy when they told him they were in the market. In his not-at-all-subtle way, Peter said they would give him their business if they both would sit down for a legitimate conversation about their situation. As they say, it was an offer he couldn't refuse.

At their kitchen table, surrounded by abandoned home improvement projects, Spencer and Diane were surprisingly forthright about their situation (perilous), their attitude (undaunted), and their debt (astronomical). "The market will turn around soon," Spencer said. "It always does. By that time, Diane will be able to supplement our income. We can put her entire salary toward our debt. In the meantime, we are paying taxes on a half-dozen houses that are in my name, but I can't afford to sell them for what they will bring right now."

"Cutbacks" were definitely in place; but as far as Peter could tell, that just meant fewer highbrow restaurants, no vacation that year, and no more buying houses. Whatever they couldn't pay for with Spencer's real estate and contracting work would go on the credit cards, which still had some room before maxing out.

Unvoiced concerns: Spencer and Diane had laid some serious groundwork in their marriage for sacrificing spiritual things in favor of material things, and their setbacks were far more likely to make it worse than make it better.

What Did Peter Tell Spencer And Diane?

☐ Sell at least half of the houses for whatever they will bring, and pay off your credit cards. Put whatever's left in retirement and college accounts. Live modestly; you might decide you like it.

☐ It disturbs me that Diane is talking about getting a job this quickly after having the kids. Give her a chance to be a mom before asking her to be a secondary breadwinner.

☐ Your financial affairs are none of my business. It sounds like a risky game, but you know far more about markets than I do. Just remember, there are more important things than money.

A Story From The Bible

The Samson and Delilah story really started long before the couple ever met—even before Samson was born. It started in Judges 13, where we read how Manoah and his wife were promised a long-awaited child, and were told that this child would grow up to honor God. But Samson did not live up to his calling—at least, not most of the time. After reading how the Spirit began to stir within him (Judges 13:25), we are immediately told that Samson sought out a woman of the Philistine to marry. "Get her," he told his father in Judges 14:3, "for she looks good to me." We assume he used the same shallow standard of judgment when he found a harlot in Gaza and eventually Delilah herself (Judges 16:1, 4)—both Philistines, both enemies of God and His people. But sometimes sin "looks good" to us.

It was not only with women that Samson had a bizarre love/hate relationship. The company of the Philistines in general seemed to have a strange appeal to him. He entertained himself with them. He gambled with them. He seems to have lashed out against them only when they did not cater to his needs, which were every bit as carnal and selfish as their own. His great victories against the Philistines described in Judges 15 only came in fits of rage. If that was the typical manner in which he "judged Israel twenty years" (Judges 15:20), it is no wonder the Philistines stayed strong enough to eventually subdue him.

Evil influences, given a comfortable place in the heart of a child of God, will eventually sap him of his spiritual strength. Delilah's betrayal could not illustrate that more perfectly. Because Samson prioritized inferior and even ungodly things, the power for good with which God had blessed him was found lacking when he needed it most. Jesus phrases it thusly in the parable of the talents: "For to everyone who has, more shall be given, and he will have an abundance; but from the one who does not have, even what he does have shall be taken away" (Matthew 25:29).

A godly outlook on life is not easily achieved or maintained. If we value the wrong things when entering into a relationship with Jesus, it is highly unlikely we will be able to fix that on the fly. It's far more likely that we will convince ourselves we can have our cake of worldliness and still eat His Supper with Him every first day of the week.

Parents can set their children up for success by practicing Proverbs 22:4 parenting (usually with a little Proverbs 23:13-14 sprinkled in). But ultimately, children will construct their own system of values. Exactly how early Samson's fascination with all things Philistine began, we are not told. Nor are we told how dutiful his parents were in steering him in more profitable directions; we know they disapproved of his first attempt at marriage (Judges 14:3), but also that they participated in the courtship ritual, at least to an extent (Judges 14:5). All parents of wayward children blame themselves for things done and left undone; that's natural. But instead of living in regret of past mistakes, we should anticipate future mistakes with a view to avoiding as many of them as possible.

For ourselves, it is impossible to improve on the simple wisdom of 1 Corinthians 15:33—"Do not be deceived: 'Bad company corrupts good morals.'" We cannot embrace the behavior and values of the world and still walk with Christ (1 John 2:15). As Paul writes in Galatians 5:16-17, "But I say, walk by the Spirit, and you will not carry out the desire of the flesh. For the flesh sets its desire against the Spirit, and the Spirit against the flesh; for these are in opposition to one another, so that you may not do the things that you please." It is the devil who tries to convince us we can live peaceably with the world, that we can indulge our tastes without regard to their spiritual repercussions. Remember, he is the "father of lies," (John 8:44).

1. Why do the things of the world "look good?" Is that always a bad thing? If not, when does what "looks good" become evil? _____

   _____

   _____

2. What safeguards can we put in place to make sure worldly things do not capture our hearts? _____

   _____

   _____

What Did Peter Tell Spencer And Diane?

☐ Sell at least half of the houses for whatever they will bring, and pay off your credit cards. Put whatever's left in retirement and college accounts. Live modestly; you might decide you like it.

☐ It disturbs me that Diane is talking about getting a job this quickly after having the kids. Give her a chance to be a mom before asking her to be a secondary breadwinner.

☑ **Your financial affairs are none of my business. It sounds like a risky game, but you know far more about markets than I do. Just remember, there are more important things than money.**

As much as we may want to tell people how to live their lives, it's a mistake to try. If a husband and wife are to "leave and cleave" with regard to their own parents, it makes little sense for us to try to micromanage their affairs—even when our personal opinions feel like they will leap from our skulls of their own accord. Judgment calls are exactly that. People do not lose their right to exercise judgment when theirs differs from mine. (If I'm specifically asked, that might be a different matter.)

My role as a brother in Christ is to encourage my brethren and/or sound a warning call, whichever may be needed. The watching and praying for such ones may, and perhaps should, intensify in times of trial. The time may come for something even stronger than that. Until then, love hopes all things.

Lesson 1a

Shopping For A Church

What Brethren Should Expect From One Another

The idea of "placing membership" with a local church is something of a modern concept. Certainly Christians who were new to an area sought out fellowship with likeminded brethren. Paul's efforts to do so in Acts 9:26-28 are a prime example. But most cities in the First Century did not have multiple congregations from which to choose; at least, we have no record to indicate otherwise. We simply read of "all the saints in Christ Jesus who are in Philippi, including the overseers and deacons" (Philippians 1:1). Clearly there was church organization. We necessarily infer that the Christians served and were cooperative in their respective roles within that organization. Furthermore, churches are required to police their membership, rooting out immorality (1 Corinthians 5:1) and factiousness (Titus 3:10). Simply being a Christian in the general area of other Christians was not enough. Spiritual camaraderie and cooperation were necessary.

In the modern day, when (for better or for worse) Christians often have options as to which body of saints to join, choices have to be made. And as with all choices, the priorities can be noble or ignoble, shallow or deep, farsighted or myopic. But if the whole point of the Spirit's work in a local fellowship is "the equipping of the saints for the work of service, to the building up of the body of Christ" (Ephesians 4:12), we will need to use the Lord's priorities and not our own to make those choices.

A Story From The Congregation

Stan and Deirdre were used to churches doing things differently than was the policy where Peter and Wendy worshiped. They missed the coffee bar, the youth program activities, the "Happy Birthday" serenades from the whole congregation. But the emphasis placed on Bible study and practical Christian living (as opposed to the feel-good, don't-condemn-anything sort of fare to which they had become accustomed) really struck a chord with them.

A sermon Peter preached one Sunday morning about the "Social Gospel" movement brought up some points they had never considered; they were not inclined to agree, Stan told Peter in the foyer afterward, but he admitted he had no Bible-based reason for disagreeing with anything Peter had said. They attended elsewhere that evening, but they were back the next Sunday morning. After a couple of months of visiting other churches and finding themselves coming back again and again, they asked for a meeting with the elders to discuss placing membership. Peter's presence was requested.

They made it quite clear immediately that, although they appreciated and agreed (at least in concept) with the emphasis the church placed on Biblical authority, they could not come around to the idea that the church was not active in any social programs. When the elders asked for specifics, they brought up charitable work and food pantries; but they always gravitated back to the "family life center." They liked the idea of having a central location where all the members could congregate for food and "fellowship" without overly burdening any individual or family. They acknowledged, though, that this sort of activity was secondary to the spread of the gospel and the spiritual instruction of the members.

Peter explained the members there were as sociable as people come (Stan and Deidre had already been in his house and the house of one of the elders). But they were careful to make a distinction between what the church sanctions and in what church members participate. "We are all in favor of Christians getting involved with charitable activities of all sorts," Peter said, "but, to borrow from 1 Timothy 5:16, 'the church must not be burdened' when the activity exceeds the mandate given to the body as an organized whole." The distinction continued to be lost on them.

Finally, Stan said, "We could keep this up all night. The bottom line is, we want to be a part of the work here. We don't want to be trouble. We will submit to the elders. But we want to be accepted. We want to be used. We don't want to be stigmatized or made to feel like pseudo-Christians. Is that going to be a problem?"

What Did Peter And The Elders Tell Stan And Deirdre?

☐ Welcome aboard. Good to have you.

☐ We will continue studying these topics from time to time, and we hope you will study along. We would be lying if we said we didn't care whether you ever came around to agreeing with us. But if you are willing to disagree without being factious about it, we won't have any issue.

☐ If a congregation is teaching error, the members of that group need to repent of that error. And in this case, repent publicly. If you are willing to renounce your previous practices, we would be glad to welcome you into fellowship. But until then, we need to keep the church pure.

A Story From The Bible

"What does the church have to offer me?" This question or the equivalent is asked by one individual or family after another as they scour the Yellow Pages for a church home. It's a seller's market, and they know it. We all know it.

Congregations, in a rush to improve their numbers, try to paint an attractive picture of themselves. They say what the prospective members want to hear, so long as they don't specifically commit to something unscriptural. But before long, a pattern of people-pleasing sets the stage for a broader concept of inclusivity. Tell enough people enough times you will give them what they want, and they will start to believe you and expect it of you.

But the solution is not to choose church leaders with firm backbones—although clearly that is a critical element in a godly church. The solution is for each of us as individuals to reassess why we are part of a congregation in the first place. Is it so that we will have a place to lead singing once a month? Or teach Bible class? Is it so our commute will be shorter and at convenient hours? Or so our children will have more peers?

Or is it so we will be better positioned to glorify God and encourage our brethren?

"Selfish ambition" sneaks in slowly, stealthily, under the guise of noble purposes. In reality, a congregation of believers from different backgrounds, experiences and ethnic groups is an ideal place for us to put Ephesians 5:21 to practical use. Unfortunately, too often it is instead a breeding ground for pride, gossip and envy.

James 3:13-18 is unequivocal, and its logic undeniable. If you have a houseful of loving, gentle people who desire their brethren's welfare first—and God's glory first of all—wonderful things will happen. "And the seed whose fruit is righteousness is sown in peace by those who make peace," (James 3:18). On the other hand, if you have a houseful of egotists, brats and opportunists, we "lie against the truth" (James 3:14). We cannot possibly honor God while pursuing dozens or even hundreds of personal agendas. It is ludicrous to even suggest such a thing. And yet this, far too often, is what we practice. And what is the result? Conflicts and quarrels. Spiritual adultery. "Therefore whoever wishes to be a friend of the world makes himself an enemy of God," (James 4:4). And if we adopt the world's values and use the world's tactics in their pursuit, who do we really think our friend is?

To paraphrase President Kennedy, "Ask not what the church can do for you; ask what you can do for the church." If the Christian life is all about service, we should seek opportunities to serve—not to be served. To borrow Paul's analogy of the body, the thumb does not seek the thumb's interests; it seeks the body's interests, and in so doing achieves its own interests.

1. What do we really "need" the church to give us? What other things do we "want" the church to give us? What is the difference? How should we respond when we get the first but not the second? _____
   _____
   _____
   _____

2. Does the squeaky wheel get the oil in the local congregation? Is that a good or a bad thing? Explain. _____

_____

_____

_____

What Did Peter And The Elders Tell Stan And Deirdre?

☑ **Welcome aboard. Good to have you.**

☑ **We will continue studying these topics from time to time, and we hope you will study along. We would be lying if we said we didn't care whether you ever came around to agreeing with us. But if you are willing to disagree without being factious about it, we won't have any issue.**

☐ If a congregation is teaching error, the members of that group need to repent of that error. And in this case, repent publicly. If you are willing to renounce your previous practices, we would be glad to welcome you into fellowship. But until then, we need to keep the church pure.

Perfection in doctrine is not a prerequisite for church membership any more than perfection in morality is. And God be praised for that; otherwise every church house would have a couple of pews full of self-righteous Pharisees congratulating themselves for how they managed to empty the building out so completely. You don't improve the hospital by getting rid of all the sick people. And you don't improve the church by getting rid of all the uninformed, misinformed, unmotivated, shallow and carnally minded people. You love them, and you teach them.

We are all learning. God is merciful to us along the way; it is strength, not weakness, when we imitate Him. Brotherly love "bears all things, believes all things, hopes all things, endures all things" (1 Corinthians 13:7). As with moral error, no one should be welcomed into fellowship who can be expected to openly embrace and publicly advocate positions condemned in Scripture. But if a Christian is willing to listen to the truth, the last thing in the world we should do is put up barriers between it and him.

Lesson 2

Equal, But Not The Same

The Roles Of Husband And Wife

Not every job in the office gets the same paycheck. Not everyone gets a corner office. But although a week without the boss may result in chaos, the same very well could be the case for the computer technician. Or the maintenance worker. Or the security guard. They are all vital to the operation. Equal, but not the same.

Husbands and wives work the same way. Few would even attempt to argue that men are somehow superior to women as examples of humanity. Yes, they are better in certain areas. But they are worse in others. Such is the case in the coming together of any two compatible humans.

God, who made us male and female, knew this from the beginning. He fully intended for husbands and wives to utilize their respective strengths in marriage, each one supplying what may be a bit lacking in the other. As a result, both the man and the woman are benefitted—and the marriage is benefitted most of all.

Denying the divinely mandated rules for marriage based on our own assessment (a flawed, human assessment at that) of our particular situation is a confession to a weak faith. We can never get closer to God's ideal for us, whether in marriage or any other application, by running from the law He has written for us. Far better for us to humbly bow to His will and apply His principles to the best of our ability, dealing with the complications and sacrifices that may ensue, than to stubbornly dig in our rebellious heels and insist that we know better than He does.

A Story From The Office

Arthur got laid off from his job. He got a good severance package and enjoyed being a full-time dad for a few months while recruiters helped him try to find a new position that suited him. They would not have minded relocating a few years ago, but Susan opened a chocolate shop downtown that was an instant sensation. She was in the process of opening a new Susan's Specialties location near their suburban home that will give her shorter commutes, and she was

Arthur and Susan
- Ages: He's 46, she's 42
- Married: 18 years
- Occupations: He's an education engineer, she's owns a candy company
- Children: 14 year old girl, Isabelle
  Problem: Income inequity

in discussions for her candy to be taken to retail outlets across the state and perhaps even further.

Arthur was genuinely delighted at Susan's success in the beginning. But after a year of watching her pay the bills, it was beginning to take a toll on his psyche. Susan was trying to maintain her regard for Arthur as the head of the family, but she found it increasingly difficult to stay silent with regard to his occasional golf outings and other indulgences. Plus she thought he could be doing a better job around the house.

When Wendy asked Susan about Arthur at church services one Sunday, she said he was on an out-of-state interview. It wasn't difficult to tell she did not approve. The next week Wendy and Peter met them both at Susan's new store to tour the facility; afterward they sat down and discussed their situation. Arthur said the job for which he applied looked promising, and that it should pay enough to fully support the family. Susan said abandoning her business at this stage was unthinkable, that she was already making as much as Arthur would make in their new job and would be making much more soon, and that she would still respect Arthur if he were to remain a "house-husband"—assuming, of course, he took a bit more pride in his work.

Unvoiced concerns: Arthur felt he had been supplanted in large measure as the head of the household; Susan felt burdened with too many roles and unappreciated in all of them.

What Did Peter And Wendy Tell Arthur And Susan?

☐ Have Arthur become the CEO of Susan's Specialties. That way he can be a productive part of her success while still being seen as the head of the family.

☐ Have Arthur continue pursuing this job and others, even if it means relocating. If he gets one, Susan can either liquidate the business or let her people run it locally while she opens a store in the family's new hometown.

☐ Encourage Arthur to accept any local work he can, even if it is out of his normal expertise, as he looks for a job locally. Who knows? He may have a real knack for furniture making.

A Story From The Bible

When the writer of Hebrews tells us by inspiration that God "spoke long ago to the fathers" (Hebrews 1:1), he was not just referring generally to their Jewish ancestry, irrespective of sex. Fathers were seen as the leaders of the family in every sense of the word. Many ancient cultures (as with many today) considered women to be inherently inferior intellectually and spiritually, treated as little more than baby-making machines. There is no reason to assume Israelite women were seen as such; great honor is showered upon women such as Deborah, Jael, Esther, and even Rahab. Even so, it is clear the Israelites respected and preserved the different roles of men and women, including the role of men as the heads of house.

In ancient culture such as theirs (and many cultures today), where women were often considered intellectually and spiritually inferior, the idea of male headship was welcomed and not questioned. In our society, women receive much more respect generally than in ancient times, which is good. But their increased importance in society has resulted in them assuming roles traditionally withheld from them.

We read in 1 Peter 3:1-4 that wives should adorn themselves with "chaste and respectful behavior," including and especially when their husbands are less than godly. Such behavior has a better chance of winning their husbands over for the Lord than insubordination, well-intentioned though it may be. Peter goes on to write in verses 5-6, "For in this way in former times the holy women also, who hoped in God, used to adorn themselves, being submissive to their own husbands; just as Sarah obeyed Abraham, calling him lord and you have become her children if you do what is right without being frightened by any fear." It is easy to make jokes about husbands requiring their wives to call them "lord" today, but the main point should not be missed: Sarah acknowledged the spiritual and practical headship of her husband, and the inspired apostle requires married women who follow Jesus today to do the same. The degree of input allowed and solicited from wives may vary somewhat from husband to husband and from culture to culture. But the general roles have been designated by God, and followers of God must accept and implement them.

Modern society, we are told, has advanced sociologically over the past few millennia, leading to a different view of marriage than existed in Bible times. "The Bible spoke to the culture of its day," the claim goes, "but our culture is different." To a certain degree, there is some validity to this. A 21st-century husband trying to bind first-century or even 17th-century mores on his wife and family will likely set himself and his family up for disaster. Even so, the general concept of male leadership is not a cultural truth but a divine truth. It dates back to the Garden of Eden (Genesis 3:16). If God had seen fit to "fix" the inequity of the sexes in Jesus, He would have done so; since when have cultural norms kept God from attempting to accomplish His will among men?

Sarah was by no means perfect in her support of Abraham. In fact, she is most famous for the instances when she was a hindrance. It was Sarah's idea to supplement God's plan for a family by bringing her handmaid, Hagar, into her husband's bed and having her bear his child (Genesis 16). The strife between the two women at the time and later, after the birth of Sarah's own son (Genesis 21:1-21), were a direct result of her own spiritual failing and Abraham's refusal to exercise spiritual headship. Still, Scripture demands that we not be too harsh with Sarah. Hebrews 11:11-12 cites her as an example of faith and implies that without that faith Isaac could not have been born and Abraham's family would have been cut off at its inception.

Wives today will not be perfect either. But by giving themselves first to God and then to their husbands, respecting the authority of both, they can deliver their own souls and contribute greatly to the salvation of their husbands, their children, and their peers.

1. How does a wife acknowledge her husband's headship if He is not a Christian? How does a husband exercise his own headship if his wife is not a Christian? _____
   _____
   _____

2. Read 1 Samuel 25. Consider the marriage of Nabal and Abigail. Clearly a wife submits to God first, even if it means rejecting her husband's wishes. But when, if ever, is it permissible for a wife to act in rebellion against her husband's judgment. _____
   _____
   _____

What Did Peter And Wendy Tell Arthur And Susan?

☐ Have Arthur become the CEO of Susan's Specialties. That way he can be a productive part of her success while still being seen as the head of the family.

☑ **Have Arthur continue pursuing this job and others, even if it means relocating. If he gets one, Susan can either liquidate the business or let her people run it locally while she opens a store in the family's new hometown.**

☑ **Encourage Arthur to accept any local work he can, even if it is out of his normal expertise, as he looks for a job locally. Who knows? He may have a real knack for furniture making.**

There's no pat answer here. But forcing Arthur into a role he is not suited for will only make Susan resent him and make Arthur feel that much more worthless.

Arthur needs to do his best to earn a living — for his own self-esteem, and to show Susan and their daughter how seriously he takes his role with the family. It may be that Arthur needs to find a new career. It may be that the family needs to relocate. An ideal situation is unlikely to present itself. Arthur and Susan need to be honest with each other regarding whether her larger paycheck will be a source of friction for them long-term. Would it be easier for him to be the head of the house and underemployed, or for her to sacrifice her burgeoning career to more fully support her husband? They may have to choose.

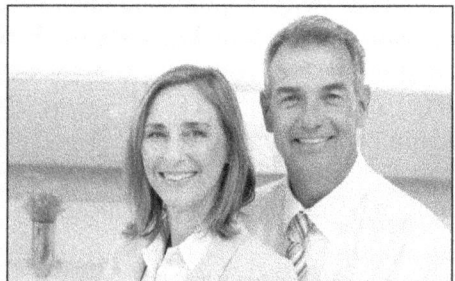

Lesson 2a

One In Christ Jesus

Male And Female Roles In The Church

An increasingly large and increasingly vocal segment of our brotherhood clamors for the inclusion of women in visible positions, including leadership positions. "Society has changed over the last 2,000 years," we are told (as though we hadn't noticed). "So must the church."

No, the church must honor its Lord. And the Lord tells us in the Spirit, "Christ is the head of every man, and the man is the head of a woman," (1 Corinthians 11:3).

The headship of husbands and the headship of Jesus go hand in hand. Many of the ones who clamor for a more equitable distribution of responsibility in the home are the ones dismissing the idea of Biblical authority. And it is only natural—marriage roles are derived from Biblical teachings; a lack of regard for those instructions can be expected to go along with a lack of regard for other instructions or for the concept of authority entirely.

Submitting to authority does not rob the individual of his or her individuality or personhood; it is a voluntary abdication of the role of head. If we cannot bring ourselves to expect wives to accept this role in the home, we are well on the road to rejecting Jesus' role as "head over all things to the church" (Ephesians 1:22).

A Story From The Congregation

Practically from the day Peter and Wendy began work with one particular congregation, they anticipated problems coming from Nate and Adele. Well, mostly Adele. Adele, naturally forceful and outspoken, was constantly outspoken with her opinions about everything, from the preaching to the Bible class curriculum to world events. Nate, her vocal counterpart, mostly kept whatever opinions he had to himself and rarely if ever disagreed with Adele.

Adele asked Peter one day if he had seen a particular website published by brethren, which promoted the position that Galatians 3:28 negated any distinction in church roles based on sex. He said he had and tried to explain why he disagreed, but she wasn't having any of it. He asked her and Nate to meet with the elders and him to discuss it further.

They met at the church building the next evening. Peter made the case that when Paul wrote, "there is neither male nor female," he was not denying the same roles he mandated in 1 Corinthians 11 and 1 Timothy 2. He was emphasizing that we don't see ourselves anymore as, first and foremost, either Jews or Gentiles, or slaves or free men, or even as men or women—that our common relationship in Jesus puts us all on equal footing. "The issue of roles is not under consideration in Galatians," Peter said. "We need to go to other passages for that. And those other passages state clearly that the roles of pulpit preacher (1 Corinthians 14:34-36) and local overseer (1 Timothy 3:2) are reserved for men.

She agreed that having female preachers and elders was out of bounds, but that it would be a harmless and much appreciated gesture toward the women of the church if a woman could be included as greeters in the foyer. "But what about communion trays?" she asked. "Most of the attendants do not lead prayers or even speak. Surely no harm could be done by including women in this simple role of service." Nate, as had been the case throughout the discussion, sat silently, nodding a bit.

What Did Peter And The Elders Tell Adele And Nate?

☐ True, most communion attendants do not fall under the heading of authority figures. Passing trays while standing and walking is no different than passing them while sitting. If we can have your assurance that no further advancement of female roles will ensue, I would have no problem with this.

☐ There is no conceivable way that the road ends here. Accepting women in this role will inevitably lead to requests for more responsibility, if not from you then from someone else. Now, if you don't mind, we would like to talk for a bit about spiritual headship in the family.

☐ The official position of the eldership has been well established for years, and we will not tolerate factiousness. Read Titus 3:10 and consider this your first warning.

A Story From The Bible

The book of Acts leaves us hanging with respect to the future of the apostle Paul. His letters to Timothy and Titus, which cannot be reconciled to the Acts story, clearly indicate that Paul was freed for a time after Acts ends. As we would have expected, Paul quickly resumed his preaching tours. He made a trip to the island of Crete, where he either started or reinforced several churches; he left Titus behind to continue the work (Titus 1:5). He also made a return trip to Ephesus and left Timothy behind when he moved on to Macedonia (1 Timothy 1:3). Given Paul's reference to Timothy's acquaintance with Onesiphorus and his actions for the Lord in Ephesus (2 Timothy 1:16-18), it is generally assumed that Timothy remained in Ephesus until he left to be with Paul during his second imprisonment.

About seven years before the writing of 1 Timothy, Paul told the men then serving as overseers in Ephesus—at least three of them, judging from Paul's use of the phrase "all of you" in Acts 20:25—that he would never see them again. Paul may simply have been mistaken; however, since the inspiration of the Spirit appears prominently in Paul's address, it seems at least possible if not likely that these men were no longer a part of the work in Ephesus by the time 1 Timothy was written. (Could the heretics Hymanaeus and Alexander, to whom Paul refers in 1 Timothy 1:20, have been two of those elders, having failed to heed Paul's warnings in their meeting in Miletus?)

In any case, whether the need in Ephesus was for a new eldership or merely more participants in the existing one, Paul wanted to make sure things were done properly in his absence. This involved two basic teachings: the proper choice of elders and deacons, which he addresses in chapter 3; and the proper behavior of such men and those who are submitting to them, which he touches on in chapters 4 and 5.

The word "qualifications" might not be the best term when referring to the character traits in 1 Timothy 3:1-7 and Titus 1:5-9. "Qualifications" implies that if a man can check off all of the indicated boxes, he is necessarily fit to serve as a congregational overseer. Such is hardly the case, even if you include aspiring to the office (from 1 Timothy 3:1) as one of the qualifications. These descriptions, which overlap greatly but are hardly identical, are composite sketches given by inspiration to the two young preachers so they will know a potential elder or deacon when they see one—much like a police sketch artist may provide a general rendering of what a suspect in a crime may look like. Is this a man given to the Lord? A family man? A man in control of his words and emotions? A man not beholden to his vices? A man who can provide spiritual leadership to the flock? If so, he should be under consideration.

Both elders and deacons are to be married to a single woman. This would clearly eliminate women from consideration in these areas. The argument that the First Century society was too unenlightened to accept a greater role for women, and that it is necessary for us in the modern day to correct the problem that went unaddressed, is circular reasoning at its worst. We are to believe God agreed with the progressives 2,000 years ago but did not empower them, and that His unspoken wishes are more authoritative than His expressed will; and we "know" God took that position because He said, "there is neither male nor female, for you are all one in Christ Jesus" (Galatians 3:28). But if that's what Paul meant in Galatians 3:28, why did he also require male headship in 1 Corinthians 11:3? And if we can reject male headship, why can we not also reject Christ's headship, affirmed in the same verse, based on some convoluted understanding of, say, Galatians 5:13?

The bottom line is, some women in the church are dissatisfied with the role given them by God. The same could be said of some men, some elders, some preachers and some teenagers. And the answer to each is the same: "Therefore humble yourselves under the mighty hand of God, that He may exalt you at the proper time" (1 Peter 5:6).

1. Does the existence of prophetesses (1 Corinthians 14:29-38, Acts 21:9) imply the legitimacy of female leadership? Why or why not? _____
   _____
   _____

2. Explain the nature of female servants of the church ("deaconesses") from Romans 16:1-2, and how or if the principle may be applied in the modern day. _____
   _____
   _____

What Did Peter And The Elders Tell Adele And Nate?

☐ True, most communion attendants do not fall under the heading of authority figures. Passing trays while standing and walking is no different than passing them while sitting. If we can have your assurance that no further advancement of female roles will ensue, I would have no problem with this.

☑ **There is no conceivable way that the road ends here. Accepting women in this role will inevitably lead to requests for more responsibility, if not from you then from someone else. Now, if you don't mind, we would like to talk for a bit about spiritual headship in the family.**

☐ The official position of the eldership has been well established for years, and we will not tolerate factiousness. Read Titus 3:10, and consider this your first warning.

There is no need to make a cordial conversation more confrontational than necessary. If no effort is being made to drum up opposition to the elders, there is probably no need for a lecture on factiousness—although it might not be a bad idea for the elders to have one at the ready in case the situation worsens.

No one fights for the right to pass out communion trays. Not even Adele, although she may have convinced herself that was what she was doing. An all-consuming desire to "serve" can be sated in any number of authorized ways. The desire here is to lead; communion trays are a gateway measure.

The bigger issue is that of their family dynamic. Naturally passive men are often drawn to naturally aggressive women. When this is the case in the marriage of Christians, both have to exercise extra care to make sure the husband is the leader—not just in theory but in practicality.

Lesson 3

The Best Kind Of Favoritism

| Putting Your Spouse Before All Others |

"Today I marry my best friend." That is part of an inscription framed and given to Tracie and me as a wedding gift from her parents. Personally, I never really felt the need for a "best friend" before I got married. As long as I had someone to play with when I wanted to play, someone to pitch in when I needed to work, that was good enough. I never felt the need to bare my soul, so the lack of someone to whom I could bare my soul was not really much of a concern.

Tracie calls that "closed-off." And she's right. She says it's a problem. And she's right again.

I'm a lot better now. It is not easy, especially for men, to expose our innermost thoughts, feelings, weaknesses and fears to someone else. And having a safe zone where such things can be shared without any concern about being rejected or thought ill of is priceless.

That is what marriage can and should be. I believe divorce is as common as it is largely because we fear being hurt. We do not allow our spouse to get too close, so when the relationship lives down to our worst expectations we do not get hurt as bad. For fear of a disastrous marriage, we doom ourselves to a mediocre marriage—at best.

We are not usually afraid to choose a favorite restaurant, or a favorite brand of clothing, or a favorite make of car. We develop a relationship over time. Everything we learn about it makes us love it even more. We come to trust in it more and more, knowing that it is possible that we will be disappointed but growing more and more confident that we will not be.

We should not be afraid to choose a favorite person.

A Story From The Office

Joel loves golf. When Peter declined one invitation, citing a prior commitment to hit the garage sales with Wendy, he chuckled and suggested they team up with Rianna, who was planning to do the same thing. He left the golf invitation open, saying he was on the course "most Saturdays."

Peter and Wendy did cross paths with Rianna later, ironically. They helped her put a couple of end tables in her SUV,

Joel and Rianna
- Ages: He's 25, she's 25
- Married: Just over one year
- Occupations: He's a financial advisor, she's an elementary school teacher
- Children: None

Problem: Divergent interests

joked a bit about a connection between their families that day seemed destined to be, and asked if she and Joel wanted to hook up later for dinner. "Sounds great," she said. "It's been a while since we did anything out together." They assumed at the time she meant the four of them together. After she left, Peter started thinking she was talking about her and Joel.

They caught up a couple of hours later and exchanged pleasantries over seafood and iced tea. Joel mentioned their recent jaunt to Asheville on their first anniversary—antiquing for her, golf for him. "I don't mean to be a wet blanket," Peter said, "but that's a strange-sounding anniversary trip. It sounds a bit like you don't really spend that much time as a couple."

"Oh, it's not that," they both said, almost in unison. "It's just that he has his things and I have mine," Rianna continued. "We spend plenty of quality time together, but we're fine on our own, too."

"Still," Wendy said, "marriage is an organism. It has to be fed. You don't build a successful marriage unless you build together. If you don't have any common interests, if you make excuses for spending lots of time apart, you put a real strain on the relationship."

They both smiled. "Thanks for your concern," Joel said. "But really, I'm happy, she's happy"—he looked at Rianna, who nodded—"we're doing fine. If other couples want to spend every waking minute together, great. We're just not that way."

Unvoiced concerns: They had very little in common, and they didn't really care; they were three years away from a divorce.

What Did Peter And Wendy Tell Joel And Rianna?

☐ Has Joel ever tried antiquing? Has Rianna ever tried golf? If so, try it again. Maybe the fifth or sixth try will be the charm.

☐ Each of you make a list of things you would be interested in doing that you have not done as a couple—cooking classes, backpacking, art, anything that could turn into a common pastime. Then compare lists and see if you can come together.

☐ A lot of young married couples start out like you. Then come the kids. Once those little feet start scurrying around the house, you will have more common interests than you will know what to do with.

A Story From The Bible

Love has a way of making a man do crazy things. Like, for instance, working for seven years for his future father-in-law for nothing more than room and board—and then, having discovered he had accidentally married the wrong sister, working for seven more. Jacob's story (Genesis 28-30) is proof. Why did Jacob cooperate with such a one-sided and duplicitous pact? Did he feel a bit guilty about his own trickery, through which he acquired his family blessing? Or did he simply love Rachel more than he resented her father? In any case, Laban managed to use the customs of his day and Jacob's cooperative attitude to get the services of his best shepherd for an extra seven years—and got both his daughters well married in the process.

Leah found herself a husband, and eventually was blessed with six sons and a daughter. But there was never any doubt that she was a poor second to her sister in Jacob's heart. This created tremendous resentment between herself and Rachel—a problem that is generally present in Bible stories when a man has more than one wife. One of them will always be the favorite, as Hannah was Elkanah's (1 Samuel 1:1-8). Rachel remained Jacob's favorite until the day she died—and her children were Jacob's favorites as well.

The point is not that bigamists should avoid favoritism. The point is, it is impossible to be "one flesh" with more than one person. It is God's design that a single man form a bond with a single woman that will be superior to, and take precedence over, any other earthly relationship. There can be only one favorite. And when we try to spread the "favorite" label around, we wind up hurting the one we are supposed to love the most—and we probably wind up hurting everyone else involved as well.

Choosing one person to marry above all others means far more than limiting one's sexual activity. It means welcoming a particular individual into the very core of one's being. Secrets are laid bare. Weaknesses are exposed—not for the purpose of emotional blackmail or one-upmanship, but to facilitate growth. A connection is created that is unparalleled and unchallenged by any other relationship, existing or future.

A wife need not be her husband's favorite in every single situation of life, nor a husband his wife's. But the more circumstances that come up where the company of another is preferred, the weaker the bond will become. This is especially the case when another of the opposite sex becomes a social or emotional rival. Many a marriage has begun to collapse with an "innocent" private conversation or lunch. Perhaps the intention at the time was not to seek intimacy with one other than one's spouse; but the seeds for infidelity were sown, and further "innocent" gestures allowed them to germinate. Had the spouse remained the one preferred, the marriage would not have been threatened.

Two people cannot get closer than "one flesh." Affection for one's marriage partner should be second nature; Paul says as much when he wrote, "He who loves his own wife loves himself; for no one ever hated his own flesh, but nourishes and cherishes it," (Ephesians 5:28-29).

1. Is there a difference between preferring the company of a same-sex friend to that of your spouse versus preferring the company of an opposite-sex friend? Explain your answer.

_____

_____

2. Under what circumstances if any should a married person enjoy the private company of a member of the opposite sex? Explain why such contact can be harmful or harmless. __

_____

_____

What Did Peter And Wendy Tell Joel And Rianna?

☐ Has Joel ever tried antiquing? Has Rianna ever tried golf? If so, try it again. Maybe the fifth or sixth try will be the charm.

☑ **Each of you make a list of things you would be interested in doing that you have not done as a couple—cooking classes, backpacking, art, anything that could turn into a common pastime. Then compare lists and see if you can come together.**

☐ A lot of young married couples start out like you. Then come the kids. Once those little feet start scurrying around the house, you will have more common interests than you will know what to do with.

Seeing children as a binder in an inadequate marriage is highly dangerous. If the marriage manages to survive the strain and stress children inevitably provide, "empty nest syndrome" will only make the gap between husband and wife that has always been there seem enormous. If we don't want "staying together for the kids" marriages, we shouldn't count on the kids to keep marriages together.

Forcing one party into the other's world likely will build resentment in both—although some couples thrive in a "let me teach you" kind of environment. The occasional solo outing is fine as long as both parties are comfortable, and as long as there is plenty of "Joel and Rianna time" as well. It doesn't matter what form that time takes, so long as they both take joy in it and each other.

Lesson 3a

Giving Preference To One Another

The Special Relationship Between Brethren

Different versions render Romans 12:10 in slightly different ways. The New American Standard Bible reads, "Be devoted to one another in brotherly love; give preference to one another in honor." The same basic impression is left in most other wordings, though: we treat brothers and sisters in Christ differently than we treat others. Better. Whether we are "preferring" their honor over our own honor or over the honor we show toward others, we wind up more or less in the same place.

We are told repeatedly to love our neighbor (Leviticus 19:18, Matthew 22:39, Galatians 5:14, etc.). Our "neighbor" even includes our enemies (Matthew 5:44, Luke 10:30-39). No human being made in the image of God deserves our contempt and disregard. But that is hardly the same as showing the brotherly love taught to us by God (1 Thessalonians 4:9), which testifies to the love we have for God Himself (1 John 4:20-21).

"There is a friend who sticks closer than a brother," Solomon writes in Proverbs 18:24. A brother in Christ is that "friend."

A Story From The Congregation

Derek concerned Peter and Wendy practically from the day they met him. He never seemed to fit in with his high school Bible class. He did not have anyone quite on his grade level. Beyond that, he was quiet to the point of sullenness, seldom participatory in—and often absent from—the social activities the kids would arrange for themselves, even exiting the church building immediately after the close of services to hole up in the back seat of his family's SUV to read or listen to his music.

The odd thing was, Claire, Peter and Wendy's 16-year-old daughter, insisted he was a completely different person at school. He socialized well with his peers and teachers, he was active in school clubs, and he had a large number of friends that kept his weekends filled. He just didn't seem to have any use at all for the other teens at church—or anyone else at church, for that matter.

Jon and Reese, on the other hand, were extremely sociable with the other church parents. And they were aware of, and somewhat frustrated at, their only child's inability to bond with other young Christians. "He just doesn't fit in with the kids at church," Reese said. She said she wanted to make sure she wasn't blaming the other kids, and then more or less went on to do exactly that. "Cliques" had developed, she said, and Derek was not included. However, the friends he had at school, while not religious for the most part, were good kids who did not get into trouble. "If he doesn't fit in at church," Jon said, "we can't make him fit in."

What Did Peter And Wendy Tell Jon And Reese?

☐ It's almost pointless to tell a teenager who his friends are supposed to be. If his friends at school do not seem to be getting Derek into trouble, count your blessings. Just make sure he attends all church functions and Bible classes. A quiet Derek is better than no Derek at all.

☐ We apologize on Claire's behalf for not getting Derek more involved. If he is willing to socialize with others, clearly we are not doing a good enough job of including him. Tell him we will do better in the future, and to seek us out when he is ready.

☐ It's tough enough keeping good Christian kids out of trouble under the best of circumstances; when they reject the good influence of their Christian brethren, it is practically impossible. Check his drawers, his backpack, his phone, his Facebook. Dollars to doughnuts, he's into something.

A Story From The Bible

We are told in no uncertain terms that "God is not one to show partiality" (Acts 10:34). And again, "there is no partiality with God," (Romans 2:11). And yet again, "God shows no partiality" (Galatians 2:6). So what are we to make of it when the Bible describes God showing partiality? And especially in such a cruel and mean-spirited (it would seem) way as He does in Malachi 1:2-3, "Yet I have loved Jacob; but I have hated Esau."

The first part of the answer is to go back to the verses cited and discuss what exactly is meant by "partiality." In Acts 10:34, Peter has come to realize that Gentiles have equal access to the gospel, that God will not reject all Gentiles simply because they have no physical stock in Abraham or spiritual stock in the Law of Moses. In Romans 2:11, Paul writes that Jews and Gentiles alike will be judged by their deeds; there will not be one standard for one group and another one, either easier or harder, for the other group. And in Galatians 2:6, Paul makes reference to the fact that people often are in the habit of regarding the opinions of some people as being more important than the opinions of others based simply on standing within human society; he says he would not have been overly impressed if the "important" people in Jerusalem had condemned his actions (they did not, by the way), because God would judge more fairly than that.

Fairness is the main consideration. God will deal fairly with mankind. No one will be lost because God did not treat him or her with equity. Likewise, no one will be saved simply because of shallow considerations such as money, popularity or family connections.

Fairness is not the issue in Malachi 1:2-3. Holiness is. The nation of Edom, like their ancestor Esau, had rejected God and His values. And as a consequence, God had condemned the

Edomites. Their culture had already begun to disappear by the time Malachi wrote, and by the end of the First Century they were extinct or all but.

Jacob, on the other hand, was a man of faith. He gave rise to a nation of faith. Jacob certainly had his failures, as did the nation. But the commitment to God seen on Jacob's side of the family tree could not be compared to that of Esau's side, even on Jacob's worst day and Esau's worst. Jacob was the favored son, both by his mother and (more importantly) by his God.

As God's favorite, he was treated differently. That's not unfairness. That's simply accepting an unrefuted spiritual reality. As Paul writes in Romans 9:19-25, God has the right to extend or withhold mercy as He chooses. And He chooses His favorite. This one disappoints his father far too often, just like his wayward brother. But God does not punish his sin. God gives him grace. As David writes in Psalm 32:1-2, "How blessed is he whose transgression is forgiven, whose sin is covered! How blessed is the man to whom the Lord does not impute iniquity, and in whose spirit there is no deceit!"

If God simply drew names out of a hat to determine the breadth of His grace, that would be partial. But He does not. He extends grace to us through faith (Ephesians 2:8). Whoever wishes to seek out, acquire, maintain and build this faith can and will be recipients of grace as well. No partiality. As we read in Romans 5:1-2, "Therefore, having been justified by faith, we have peace with God through our Lord Jesus Christ, through whom we also have obtained our introduction by faith into this grace in which we stand."

God had a different attitude toward faithful Jacob than He did toward unfaithful Esau. Jacob was His favorite, and He treated him accordingly. Today the people of God are "a chosen race...a people for God's own possession" (1 Peter 2:9). He does not treat us as He treats the people of the world. And thank Him for that.

1. Do people in the United States and other developed countries have an advantage over other countries with regard to access to the gospel? Why or why not? _____
   _____
   _____
   _____

2. Do people who are born to parents who are Christians have an advantage over other people with regard to building faith? Why or why not? _____
   _____
   _____
   _____

What Did Peter And Wendy Tell Jon And Reese?

☑ **It's almost pointless to tell a teenager who his friends are supposed to be. If his friends at school do not seem to be getting Derek into trouble, count your blessings. Just make sure he attends all church functions and Bible classes. A quiet Derek is better than no Derek at all.**

☐ We apologize on Claire's behalf for not getting Derek more involved. If he is willing to socialize with others, clearly we are not doing a good enough job of including him. Tell him we will do better in the future, and to seek us out when he is ready.

☐ It's tough enough keeping good Christian kids out of trouble under the best of circumstances; when they reject the good influence of their Christian brethren, it is practically impossible. Check his drawers, his backpack, his phone, his Facebook. Dollars to doughnuts, he's into something.

I am absolutely in favor of random checks of children's (including and especially teens') social media, backpacks and underwear drawers. My children have absolutely no privacy rights in my house, and they know that. That said, mere estrangement from Christian peers and attachment to worldly peers are not necessarily signs of trouble. If Derek was brought up right (and we assume he was), he should be prepared to make good decisions in the clutch. I'm certainly not going to tell his parents that he's not.

Teens socialize in different ways. It is reasonable to require them to at least go through the motions of getting along, and to be polite and respectful when they do. Certainly do not blame the other kids and parents for your own child's social awkwardness; that only feeds the notion that their isolation is forced upon them by others and that they have no control. They have plenty of control. They just need to figure out how best to exercise it.

Cutting off friendships at the knees, especially when there are not relationships with Christians to slip quickly into their places, will likely do more harm than good. Be alert for any indication of rebellion and mischief, but save the nuclear armament for when it is actually needed. And you will know when it is needed.

Lesson 4

One Flesh

Coming Together As Husband And Wife

Marriage is any number of things to any number of people—a tax status, a legal arrangement, a compromise. But to the people of God, marriage should mean one thing above all—"one flesh." That marvelous characterization given to us in Genesis 2:24 at the institution of marriage characterizes the institution of marriage better than any philosophy of man ever can.

"One flesh," obviously, has reference on the surface to the sexual conjunction of man and woman. The sex act is far more than carnal gratification. Unfortunately, the mockery that sex has become in our society clouds the beauty of God's creation. Sex without a real and permanent bond robs the participants of its true purpose—the emotional joining of two souls in a single direction.

The sex act is only an outward representation of the true connection taking place. When a man and woman come together in marriage, they create a unity that is greater than the sum of its parts. They now operate as one, not as two individuals. What is good for one is good for both. They do not compete against one another any more than a bolt would compete against its corresponding nut.

It is not surprising, considering the role of sex in the husband-wife relationship, that marital problems frequently demonstrate themselves most prominently in the bedroom. The lack of sexual activity is not the problem; it is merely the symptom of a much deeper problem—the failure, conscious or unconscious, to pursue the true and deeper unity of the flesh.

A Story From The Office

Wendy, like many preacher's wives, just has that ability to get people to talk about their problems to her—whether Wendy wants them to or not! Such was the case with Emily. The two of them had scheduled lunch after Evan started kindergarten. Wendy was hoping to hear about how Emily was more available to teach Bible classes at church. What she heard instead was far too many details about Emily and Aaron's sex life. Or lack thereof.

Aaron and Emily
· Ages: He's 32, she's 31
· Married: 9 years
· Occupations: He's a building contractor, she's a homemaker
· Children: 5 year old boy, Evan
Problem: Lack of intimacy

Peter and Wendy had them both over for lunch the next Sunday, and somehow they managed to gracefully broach the subject of their marriage. Claire entertained Evan for two hours while the four adults sat at the dining room table, the remains of Wendy's famous paella still in front of them, discussing their situation.

Emily's position was that Aaron's commute and long hours had him leaving the house around daybreak, coming home barely in time for dinner, and going to bed before 10. She said he spent most of his evening hours watching television. The weekends tended to be eaten up with church activities and social engagements.

Aaron claimed to be equally frustrated. He said he didn't feel like being romantic while Evan was still awake, that the weekend social engagements were mostly of Emily's making, and that she rebuffed him as often as not when he did express interest.

Unvoiced concerns: Emily feared Aaron is filling her role in other ways—perhaps pornography, perhaps even the beginnings of an affair; Aaron thought Emily is selfish and inconsiderate of his efforts to provide for the family, and that no amount of attention would be adequate for her.

What Did Peter And Wendy Tell Aaron And Emily?

☐ Sex is not the measurement for how successful a marriage is. Fixating on fleshly concerns is only forcing a separation between the two of you.

☐ If Emily were to find a job outside the home, she might be able to let Aaron spend fewer hours at his job; perhaps they could even start putting some money away for a getaway weekend.

☐ Cut back on the socializing if you have to. Drop Evan with a babysitter for two or three nights a month and go on a "date" at the house. Less sleep, more coffee!

A Story From The Bible

A marriage, in a nutshell, is what God says it is. When you want to know the laws for the United States, you go to the U.S. Constitution; that is the standard. When you want to know the laws for card games, you go to Hoyle; that is the standard. And when you want to know the laws for marriage, you go to the standard left to us by the One who created both mankind and marriage—the Bible.

The story of the first marriage is told completely in about a page of text in most Bibles. But in that brief narrative in Genesis 2-4 we are given a remarkable amount of information about the nature of marriage.

It comes from God. God made man. Then He made woman for man. She was particularly appropriate for man's need—"a helper suitable for him" (Genesis 2:20). God, being all-powerful, could have made man self-sufficient. But He wanted Adam and all his sons to be not only individual units but also part of a greater one.

It involves one man and one woman. This rule has not been consistently followed, even by the people of God. Still, the simple truth that was pronounced in the beginning cannot be denied—one man, one woman, one lifetime. "Male and female He created them" (Genesis 1:27); homosexuality, by its very nature, is contrary to God's design (Romans 1:26-27). Polygamy and polyamory also violate this principle.

It separates a married couple from all others, including family. The "one flesh" (Genesis 2:24) created in marriage excludes all others. The husband and wife become a single unit, as symbolized and realized in the sexual bond. They have a bond between themselves that supersedes all others, with the sole exception of their connection to Jesus Christ (Luke 14:26).

It is God's design for producing children. Not all marriages produce children, of course. And some parents do their job exceedingly well while remaining single. Still, God intentionally made humans in such a way as to require both a father and a mother. And just as this is the only way a child can be brought into the world, so also it is the best way to bring a child up in the world.

It produces an innocent nakedness. All is laid bare, both literally and figuratively, before one's spouse, and without shame. Certain subject matters, personal feelings and (obviously) body parts are not to be paraded before mankind; such a lack of self-control is a demonstration of an absence of Christ in our hearts. But the deepest secrets of our heart should be laid open to the one with whom we are "one flesh." Sin, although certainly shameful before God, should be discussed without arrogance or inhibition. Who better to hear our confession of sin and prayer for forgiveness (James 5:16) better than a husband or wife?

The assumption in all these matters is that God knows best how marriage should operate. If we are willing to trust in Him as the Giver of "every perfect gift" (James 1:17), we should thank Him for this gift and use it in the way He intended—and we should respect the revelation of His will in this matter as much as we do in any other matter.

1. Do the laws of men impact how we should define and implement marriage as God's people? Explain why or why not. _____
   _____
   _____

2. Do Old Testament examples of divorce or multiple marriages impact the teachings of Christ for us in Matthew 19 and other New Testament passages? Explain your answer.
   _____
   _____

What Did Peter And Wendy Tell Aaron And Emily?

☐ Sex is not the measurement for how successful a marriage is. Fixating on fleshly concerns is only forcing a separation between the two of you.

☐ If Emily were to find a job outside the home, she might be able to let Aaron spend fewer hours at his job; perhaps they could even start putting some money away for a getaway weekend.

☑ **Cut back on the socializing if you have to. Drop Evan with a babysitter for two or three nights a month and go on a "date" at the house. Less sleep, more coffee!**

It's counterproductive to deny the importance of intimacy in a marriage, including and particularly sexual intimacy. That intimacy may be shown in different ways and with different frequency as we grow older, but it must be shown.

Blaming one party for hours worked or another for hours not worked dodges the issue. The problem is not money, or even time; it's priorities. Choosing to cordon off time in the week for maintaining and building a relationship is a sign of commitment. Your spouse will appreciate it, and probably reciprocate.

Lesson 4a

The Body Of Christ

The Nature Of Spiritual Fellowship

God makes husbands and wives "one flesh." A union is created in marriage that has identity beyond the individual humans involved. A "they" exists where once there was just a "he" and a "she."

The same thing happens in the Lord's church, "which is His body" (Ephesians 1:23). As with husbands and wives, the individual component members of the church continue to exist and function individually. Their humanity, and particularly their accountability before God, remain unchanged. But now there is a new element—a union of the parts, which has identity of its own.

As with marriage—and indeed, all things—God's rules must apply. If we are prepared to submit to His rules with regard to marriage, we also must accept His teaching with regard to the bride of Christ and our part in it.

God decides who is included. It is not our place to declare ourselves married to the Lord. We must accept His spiritual proposal in His way. He is the husband, and "the head of every man" (1 Corinthians 11:3). Simply praying a particular prayer, or making a public commitment of some sort, or feeling something within your heart—these are not part of God's wedding ceremony. Imagine the mockery (and, ultimately, the legal proceedings) that would ensue if I were to declare myself married to Jennifer Aniston or my wife to Donald Trump—and thus entitled to all the benefits that come with such a marriage! How does it become any less ridiculous, or actionable, when we simply pronounce ourselves married to the Lord?

God decides who is excluded. The divine marriage ceremony described in Revelation 21 leaves out "the cowardly and unbelieving and abominable and murderers and immoral persons and sorcerers and idolaters and all liars" (Revelation 21:8). We would not likely approve of such ones being married to our sons and daughters; we should not be sur-prised if the Heavenly Father requires a better match for His Son. We are called in 1 Peter 2:9 "a chosen race, a royal priesthood a holy nation, a people for God's own possession." We cannot bring glory to His family by trying to force Him to accept undesirables (as He defines undesirable).

God decides when and if an excluded one can become included. We are saved by grace (Ephesians 2:8). Only by God choosing us can we have any hope of salvation; without that grace, we are all doomed. Since God does the saving and the choosing, He also sets the standards by which one will be saved and chosen. Emphasizing such prerequisites—including baptism (Mark 16:16)—does not diminish grace in the slightest. What diminishes grace is our insistence that we can behave in a way we think suits a child of God and then expect God will save us despite His promise not to do so (2 Thessalonians 1:8).

God decides when and if an included one can become excluded. Just as husbands and wives can conduct themselves in such a way as to make themselves unsuitable spouses, so also the children of God can fall from grace (Galatians 5:4). It is not our place to state the point at which God will cease fellowship with His people; He knows the hearts of men far better than we do. But to insist that a partaker in salvation cannot possibly find himself in "the gall of bitterness and the bondage of iniquity" (Acts 8:23) is to deny the consistent teachings of Scripture.

A Story From The Congregation

The elders called Peter into a meeting regarding Alec. He was not surprised. Alec had been visiting for a couple of months and had indicated an interest in placing membership. But Peter had realized through brief discussions with him in the foyer after services that Alec had been brought up in a denomination. Baptism was practiced after a fashion, but the group was certainly not known for believing in baptism as an essential part of the forgiveness process as indicated in passages such as Mark 16:16, Acts 22:16 and 1 Peter 3:21.

Alec had insisted to the elders that at the time of his "conversion" (he was 21 at the time), he was immersed in water. He said he understood it at the time to be for the exact purpose given it in Scripture—"for the forgiveness of your sins" (Acts 2:38). "I have no doubt at all of my salvation," Alec said. "What I read about in Scripture, that's exactly what I did."

The elders were skeptical. They knew how people can tend to remember what they want to remember. Could it be that Alec found the truth despite the best efforts of his spiritual advisors at the time, who no doubt considered baptism to be administered after salvation? Could they welcome into fellowship someone who has not had his sins washed away in the manner proscribed by the New Testament?

What Did Peter Tell The Elders?

☐ Decisions like this are why we have elders. I trust your judgment, and so does the church. If you believe Alec is saved, welcome him. If not, require him to be baptized.

☐ It is not possible for someone to have experienced what he says he experienced. If he was not taught the truth, he could not have responded to the truth. And there's no reason to think he was taught the truth.

☐ Some of the members would probably have a problem with his current status if they knew about it. If they don't know, maybe that's for the best. If some do know, feel them out and see where they stand.

A Story From The Bible

Paul stayed in Ephesus only briefly during his first preaching tour. Acts 18:18-21 describes how he met with the Jews in the synagogue only once before continuing on his way back to Jerusalem. No mention is made of any converts. Clearly, though, there came to be converts in the near future—no doubt largely as a result of the work of Paul's good friends and occasional business partners, Aquila and Priscilla.

Acts 18 concludes with a record of their work with a preacher named Apollos, a man who knew enough about Jesus to preach Him publicly and boldly but not well enough to know the difference between His baptism and John's. His enthusiasm and faith were admirable, but poorly grounded. So Aquila and Priscilla "took him aside and explained to him the way of God more accurately" (Acts 18:26). Clearly this would at least include baptism in the name of Jesus, as required by the apostles on the day of Pentecost (Acts 2:38) and ever since (Acts 10:48, etc.). It appears Apollos had happened upon John during his brief ministry, and perhaps even been turned to Jesus as was the case with many of John's disciples (John 1:29-34); presumably he was baptized by John as testimony to his faith and was baptizing others similarly. But Apollos did not know the mandate given by the Spirit that believers in Jesus were to be baptized in His name, and that only such obedient believers would be added to His church (Acts 2:47). Aquila and Priscilla appreciated Apollos' zeal, but they did not want him to remain ignorant.

John was preaching "a baptism of repentance for the forgiveness of sins" (Mark 1:4). The text is unclear as to whether a recipient of such a baptism would be required to be baptized again (and have his sins forgiven again) in Jesus. If we were told specifically whether Apollos was baptized again in Ephesus, it would clear up this fine point; as it is, we are not told. In any case, it is a moot point for us. Clearly today, anyone who would have his sins remitted must submit to baptism for forgiveness of sins (Mark 16:16, Acts 22:16, etc.). The only such baptism available to us is baptism in the name of Jesus.

When Paul returned to Ephesus on his third tour, he found twelve men claiming to be disciples (Acts 19:7). Perhaps themselves students of Apollos in his earlier years, they knew only of the baptism of John; they did not even know of the coming of the Holy Spirit upon the apostles, as recorded in Acts 2. These ones were baptized by Paul, at which time he laid hands on them so they would receive the gift of the Spirit themselves. Clearly, whether Apollos received baptism in Ephesus or not, these twelve disciples needed to be baptized. Perhaps they had received John's baptism after Pentecost, when it was of no effect; perhaps all of John's disciples, including Apollos and even the apostles themselves, were required to be baptized in Jesus regardless of their response to John's preaching.

Both circumstances demonstrate that membership in the body of Christ cannot simply be claimed. One must accept the gospel He and His disciples taught, and respond in the way He and His disciples required believers to respond—in water baptism for remission of sins in the name of Jesus.

1. Does a true disciple of Jesus need to be baptized again if he finds himself in error with regard to a point of doctrine? Explain your answer. _____

_____

_____

_____

2. What implications, if any, would the story of the twelve Ephesian disciples have with regard to someone who went through a form of baptism in a denomination? _____

_____

_____

_____

What Did Peter Tell The Elders?

☑ **Decisions like this are why we have elders. I trust your judgment, and so does the church. If you believe Alec is saved, welcome him. If not, require him to be baptized.**

☐ It is not possible for someone to have experienced what he says he experienced. If he was not taught the truth, he could not have responded to the truth. And there's no reason to think he was taught the truth.

☐ Some of the members would probably have a problem with his current status if they knew about it. If they don't know, maybe that's for the best. If some do know, feel them out and see where they stand.

It insults the power of the gospel, and inappropriately elevates the importance of the preacher, to think a soul seeking for truth cannot simply pick up his Bible and find it. Countless souls have done exactly that over the years; it is not the place of someone who was not there to tell Alec he is not one of those souls.

Elders are not needed for doctrinal decisions; those have already been made by the Lord. We need elders for their judgment in matters that do not appear black and white. They must lead. Elders who hesitate to lead because of possible reactions from members or unpopularity from outsiders should not be serving as elders in the first place.

Lesson 5

True Commitment

Saying Yes When You Want To Say No (And Vice Versa)

The teachings of Matthew 19:3-12 with regard to marriage, divorce and possible remarriage are among the least ambiguous in the text. Verse 6 reads, "What therefore God has joined together, let no man separate." Verse 9 reads, "whoever divorces his wife, except for immorality, and marries another woman commits adultery." As the saying goes, you would need help to misunderstand that. Unfortunately, help is available. People come from all over, including from among the people of God, to tell us that divorce is not bad, that remarriage is not prohibited, that society's rules and standards should hold sway instead of God's revealed will.

It should be noted, though, Jesus addressed both the root cause of the diversion from the truth and the ultimate solution He offers for people caught in seemingly untenable situations—circumstances that would seem to render Jesus' simple instructions as irrelevant or even dangerous. He speaks to the root cause in verse 11, "Not all men can accept this statement, but only those to whom it has been given." It is not only understandable that people would reject Jesus' teachings, it is predictable. People who are not called by the gospel to live in Jesus (2 Thessalonians 2:14) should not be expected to exercise this sort of restraint. Only a commitment to Jesus could compel someone to obey Jesus at all times; consequently, sinners are quite likely to reject His teaching. But the attitude of the rebellious, sinful majority should not have any bearing on the behavior of those who claim to be Christians.

With regard to the solution, He says in verse 12, "there are also eunuchs who made themselves eunuchs for the sake of the kingdom of heaven." In blunt terms, some will be called upon to restrain themselves sexually—even for the rest of their lives. We sympathize greatly with such ones. But we say to them the same thing we say to a homosexual who is battling sinful urges in his attempts to walk with Christ, or a person who can't find "the right one" and wishes to find satisfaction in pornography: your predisposition, your background, your desires, your circumstances, these are not excuses for rejecting the will of God in your life. If you cannot have sex in an approved husband-wife relationship, you cannot have sex at all.

He concludes His argument by saying, "He who is able to accept this, let him accept it." The person of faith will do exactly that; the self-willed and faithless will not. It is as the prophet of old wrote—"For the ways of the Lord are right, and the righteous will walk in them, but transgressors will stumble in them" (Hosea 14:9).

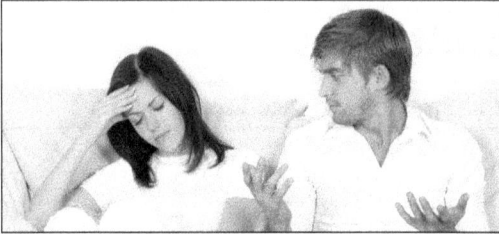

Louis and Winona
· Ages: He's 24, she's 24
· Married: 2 years
· Occupations: He's a technical writer, she's a student
· Children: None
Problem: Constant fighting

A Story From The Office

Louis and Winona were fighting again. It had gotten to be relatively obvious to anyone who knew them well. As frequent visitors to the preacher's house (they shared a passion for bridge), their quirks and mannerisms had become familiar to Peter and Wendy, even when they tried to hide them. And in one remarkable evening's exchange, they quit hiding them.

It all came out in a torrent. He was too controlling. She was a terrible house-keeper. He always called her stupid. She was stupid. He wouldn't do anything with her that she enjoyed. She nagged constantly. He had physically threatened her once. She had thrown a coffee cup at his head twice. Finally, as they both managed to take a breath at the same time, Peter and Wendy sat them down on the couch together. They gave Claire the car keys and movie money, pulled up a couple of chairs for themselves, and leaned in over the coffee table. "We've waited for you two to ask us for help ever since we met you," Peter said. "Now you're going to get some whether you want it or not."

The conversation calmed down considerably after that. Rules for the discussion were established and enforced: only one of them was allowed to talk at a time, for no more than two minutes; a raised voice from one of them drew a raised hand from one of us. It became clear right away that, despite the tempestuous nature of their relationship, genuine love was there. They wanted the marriage to work; they just didn't know how to go about making it work.

Unvoiced concern: The fighting had become a habit they might not ever be able to break.

What Did Peter And Wendy Tell Louis And Winona?

☐ Start carrying a notepad around the house. Make a tally mark every time the other one says or does something unloving. Share notes at the end of the week. I'll bet you will both be shocked at how horribly you have been treating each other.

☐ Don't act ugly. Just don't. A conversation can be lively and emotional, even to the point of "fighting." But if it ceases to be productive because of word choices or tone of voice, walk away. Finish it later, but make sure to finish before the end of the day. Then make up properly.

☐ It may be time for a 1 Corinthians 7:5-style temporary separation. Go to neutral corners for a week or so to remind yourselves how wonderful your spouse is and how wonderful your marriage can be. Pray without ceasing, and try it again.

A Story From The Bible

"Remember Lot's wife." We are never told her name. Her complete story is told in less than a single chapter of the Bible. And yet, thanks in large part to the Lord's words in Luke 17:32, she will live forever as an example of what happens to someone who thinks twice about receiving the grace of God at the expense of the things of this worldly life.

Genesis 19 tells the story of how Lot was warned by two angels that the city of Sodom, along with the other cities of the plain, were to be destroyed by the wrath of God because of their sinful behavior. The treatment the Sodomites tried to give the angels was an ample demonstration of that behavior. "Righteous Lot, oppressed by the sensual conduct of unprincipled men" (2 Peter 2:7) was ready and eager to heed the angels' warnings—perhaps having long since regretted his decision to pitch his tents toward Sodom (Genesis 13:12). But his family was difficult to convince. The men espoused to his daughters refused to take Lot seriously and stayed behind. Eventually the angels had to practically drag them to safety, so great was their love for their carnal surroundings.

The symbolism behind the angels' warnings in verse 17, "Do not look behind you," is easy to understand. "Don't look back" is a common phrase even today to refer to a decision that should be made and not regretted or reconsidered. There was nothing in Sodom that Lot's family needed. Yes, there were morally neutral things they would never see again, but faith in God is sufficient for the true believer to find contentment in any state (Philippians 4:12). Clearly God saw a backward look as a sign of regret, of doubt.

Lot's wife "looked back, and she became a pillar of salt" (Genesis 19:26). She would remain forever frozen, staring over her shoulder at the choice she made. She loved Sodom more than she trusted God. And, through the power of inspiration and the preservation of the Bible, she stands in place even today as a warning to us. Yes, commitment to God comes with a price; all things of true value do. But doubt comes with a price as well—a price we absolutely do not want to pay.

Marriage is an "all in" proposition. There are no trial marriages. There are no exit strategies. Presiding officials at weddings often say, "Marriage is not to be entered into lightly." Ignoring that advice has caused many couples to enter marriage prematurely, based on shallow impulses and not deep-seated love and connection. Even when Christians marry, bringing with them a common faith, the challenges marriage inevitably brings may cause them to look back longingly at the life they left.

There's no point in pretending marriage doesn't come at a cost. When you choose to share your entire life with another person, compromises will have to be made—from where you will get pizza on Friday night to where you will buy a house. Persisting in the habits of your old single life—or giving them up grudgingly—inevitably leads to discontent. Blame is assessed. "A better person would not ask me to give this up." No, a better person would want to give it up to serve the interests of his or her marriage.

If you are not ready to give up the freedoms of life outside of marriage, don't get married. But think long and hard. Spend time around godly couples. You may find what you are missing is more desirable than what you are clinging to.

1. What should we do if we find ourselves regretting our decision to get married? _____
_____
_____
_____

2. Should a husband and wife try to balance out who gets his or her way more often? If so, how should that be done? If not, why not? _____
_____
_____
_____

What Did Peter And Wendy Tell Louis And Winona?

☐ Start carrying a notepad around the house. Make a tally mark every time the other one says or does something unloving. Share notes at the end of the week. I'll bet you will both be shocked at how horribly you have been treating each other.

☑ **Don't act ugly. Just don't. A conversation can be lively and emotional, even to the point of "fighting." But if it ceases to be productive because of word choices or tone of voice, walk away. Finish it later, but make sure to finish before the end of the day. Then make up properly.**

☐ It may be time for a 1 Corinthians 7:5-style temporary separation. Go to neutral corners for a week or so to remind yourselves how wonderful your spouse is and how wonderful your marriage can be. Pray without ceasing, and try it again.

Keeping record of one another's wrongdoing is just about the worst thing you can do. If it's not a specific violation of the "does not take into account a wrong suffered" part of 1 Corinthians 13:5, it's pretty close.

I never counsel a couple to separate, even temporarily. It may be necessary at times, but that should come from them, not me. Nine times out of ten, problems are best worked out together. Books and articles on "fair fighting" can be helpful in teaching couples how to phrase objections in an acceptable way.

Remember, "love covers a multitude of sins" (1 Peter 4:8). Working on the love will make it easier to work on the problems.

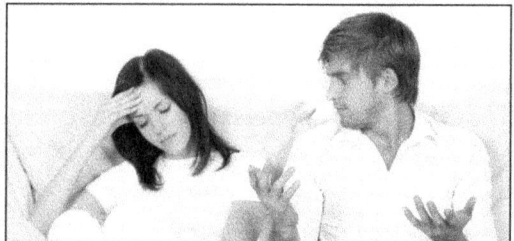

Lesson 5a

The Depth Of Discipleship

Moving Onward, Moving Upward

Jesus certainly worked hard to get people to quit following Him. He chased away the ones who ate of the loaves and fishes and then came back for more (John 6:26-27, 66). He chose figures of speech that would confuse and discourage most of His hearers, and then rejoiced when it worked (Matthew 13:10-17). Hardly the actions of someone trying to establish a kingdom.

But then, as He told Pilate, "My kingdom is not of this world" (John 18:36). Its success did not depend on raw numbers, or armament, or tactics, or any other metric used by those who pursue earthly kingdoms and earthly success. The success of His kingdom depended entirely upon the King. And He knew He would ultimately triumph, just as it was prophesied in Daniel 2:44 and any number of other Old Testament passages.

Since the success of the kingdom has no root whatsoever in His disciples, He is free to ignore quantity and focus entirely on quality. That is not to say He is indifferent to quantity; He is "not wishing for any to perish but for all to come to repentance" (2 Peter 3:9). But He is in position to accept true believers and only true believers. Those who do not pass the test are rejected. And although we may be discouraged with the relatively small number of people walking with us in His straight way (Proverbs 3:6), He is not. He has always been able "to save by many or by few" (1 Samuel 14:6). Perhaps we, like Gideon, need to be reminded how small our power is and how great His deliverance is.

The greatness of our task, the unpopularity of our calling, the price He asks us to pay—all of these can become causes for us to look back at the world. But in our hours of strength, we know the folly of that. So clearly, we need to have as many hours of strength as we can manage, and make the most of them. Jesus says, in Luke 9:62—"No one, after putting his hand to the plow and looking back, is fit for the kingdom of God." Count the cost of discipleship first, as He advises in Luke 14:28. Then, if you believe, act decisively on that belief. Measure twice, cut once.

A Story From The Congregation

When Lucas came forward during the invitation song, Peter knew why. It was for the same thing as the last time, and the time before. Drug addiction is a terrible cross to bear. And Lucas didn't always bear it well.

Lucas came from a good home. His father served as a deacon until stepping down to focus his attention on his family. His older brother had continued his straight-A and straight-arrow ways throughout college and was continuing the same pattern in law school. Lucas, though, was always troublesome. He always managed to find the wrong crowd to hang out with, always pushed his boundaries. He was fundamentally a good kid. He would give you the shirt off his back. He just would give considerably more than that for a fix.

He looked awful. He looked like he hadn't slept in days or had a decent meal in a week (which, it turned out, he hadn't). This made the third phone call from the gutter his parents had received in five years—each one in the middle of the night, each one full of sobbing, each one with pleas for help and a commitment to get cleaned up. The first time was "just" marijuana, "just" an experiment his new college friends had pushed him into. The second was heroin, and it prompted his parents to put him in a rehab clinic. He walked away halfway through his treatment and re-enrolled in college, claiming to have kicked the habit. And for six months, it looked like he had. This time, he confirmed to Peter on the front row, it was heroin again.

His parents had told Peter ahead of time that he was back at home and likely to come forward that morning, so he wasn't taken by surprise. And he was impressed with Lucas' attitude, and with the words in the letter he had Peter read to the congregation. He was deeply apologetic. He had only delayed going back to rehab so he could confess fault to the church first, and was checking in first thing Monday morning—this time to stay for the duration.

Then again, he had been impressive the first two times.

What Did Peter Tell Lucas?

☐ God forgives you, and we forgive you. It will be a tough path, as you well know, but we will be walking beside you in it, every step of the way.

☐ At some point, we need to see "fruits worthy of repentance." And this is that point. Get back in rehab. Finish it this time. Then come back. We will be thrilled to welcome you then.

☐ The damage you have done to the church's reputation cannot be undone simply by saying you're sorry. While we wait for you to get cleaned up, we will not consider you a member of the congregation here. We hope and pray we can re-establish fellowship with you in due course of time.

A Story From The Bible

The chicken is involved in breakfast. The pig is committed. In the same manner, some Christians may content themselves with simply being caught up in the outward trappings of Christianity without truly giving themselves to the Lord. Jesus referred to such ones as rocky soil in the parable of the sower, and says they tend to fall away during times of temptation (Luke 8:13). The good soil, however, although it will disappoint from time to time, is going to give all it has to the seed that has been planted in it.

A stumbling block can easily become a stepping stone for someone who is more interested in connecting with Jesus than with the world. The big decisions and moral crossroads of life separate the true disciples from the hangers-on—not based on the results of the temptation, but rather on the direction taken. One may make the right choice and do well; one may make the wrong choice and do poorly. But one may also make the right choice and do poorly. And that leads to another crossroads, where we decide whether to learn from our mistakes or to retreat from our commitment.

Jesus spoke to some would-be disciples at the first crossroads in Luke 9:59-62. Claiming to have a desire to be with the Lord, two of them wanted to place conditions on their discipleship—conditions that we might consider to be more than reasonable. But Jesus would have none of that. You are at the crossroads now, not later, He insinuates. Decide now. Don't put your hand to the plow and then look back. The same dilemma confronted the rich young ruler in Luke 18:18-23. He counted the cost and decided, with much regret, he was not up to the challenge.

Peter and Judas meet down the road at the other crossroads. Having chosen to walk with Jesus, they found out things about themselves they did not want to know. Peter's faith had a tendency to fail him at critical junctures; Judas' love of money hindered him from giving his whole heart to the Lord. But Peter did not quit on himself or his faith. He continued pursuing the Lord despite his failures. Judas indulged his vices and wound up destroying himself.

Jesus knew Peter was capable of rising from the ashes of failure. He told him in Luke 22:31-32, "Simon, Simon, behold, Satan has demanded permission to sift you like wheat; but I have prayed for you, that your faith may not fail; and you, when once you have turned again, strengthen your brothers." Exactly how unusual Satan's demand was, whether it was similar to his requests regarding Job (Job 1:9-11, 2:4-5), how common this request is in the modern day—these are questions that must go largely unanswered for now. It is enough, though, to say that Satan still has plenty of "flaming arrows" (Ephesians 6:16) left in his quiver, and that each of us is a target. Jesus even seemed to indicate prior knowledge of Peter's failings in the courtyard of the high priest early the next morning. But He knew Peter would be able to learn from that experience and allow his own failure to lead to success in others. In the same way, we know we will fall short from time to time. But that is not the same thing as losing our faith. John writes in a four-verse span both that the one who has fellowship with Jesus cannot walk in darkness and that Christians lie when they say they do not sin (1 John 1:6-9). This is no contradiction; it is an acknowledgement that we commit to a godly lifestyle, or "walk," when we come to Christ, but that walk will not be perfect. That is why we "test yourselves" (2 Corinthians 13:5) along the way—to find our level of commitment instead of allowing circumstances to reveal it.

The beauty of this arrangement is perhaps best described in Psalm 37:23-24, "The steps of a man are established by the Lord, and He delights in his way. When he falls, he will not be hurled headlong, because the Lord is the One who holds his hand." If we continue to have enough faith to hold His hand, He will continue to bear us up in our failings. It would be better, clearly, for us to walk on water every day with Jesus; but if we can't, at least we know He is there to pull us out of the water when we need Him the most.

1. What are some other examples of people whose faith failed them? Were they able to overcome? _____

_____

_____

2. Explain how "no one who is born of God sins; but He who was born of God keeps him, and the evil one does not touch him" (1 John 5:18), especially in the context of our need for an Advocate (1 John 2:1-2). _____

_____

_____

What Did Peter Tell Lucas?

☑ **God forgives you, and we forgive you. It will be a tough path, as you well know, but we will be walking beside you in it, every step of the way.**

☐ At some point, we need to see "fruits worthy of repentance." And this is that point. Get back in rehab. Finish it this time. Then come back. We will be thrilled to welcome you then.

☐ The damage you have done to the church's reputation cannot be undone simply by saying you're sorry. While we wait for you to get cleaned up, we will not consider you a member of the congregation here. We hope and pray we can re-establish fellowship with you in due course of time.

None of us gets it right the first time—or the second, or the third. Failure, even colossal failure, is not necessarily a sign of a lack of commitment. Let him who never repeated a mistake cast the first stone.

The details of the dealings with outward symptoms of sin are a family matter; the church is not involved, although certainly the elders should be a resource for wisdom should the family need one. The church is a spiritual organization. It deals with the spiritual root of its members' trials. The root is sin. The cure is Jesus. The prescription is repentance.

As often as we may read Jesus' admonition to forgive "seventy times seven," we are hard pressed to make it past one—especially when the sin in question is something foreign to us, something "we would never do." Certainly we should look for outward signs that repentance is real. But that's what front pews are for.

Imposing our human judgment as a standard for fellowship usurps God's role. If godly sorrow that works repentance is good enough for Him (2 Corinthians 2:5-11), it should be good enough for us.

Lesson 6

For Better...

Spiritual Partnership, The Way It Should Be

If "unequally yoked" is a bad thing, then "equally yoked" must be a good thing. And that's what happens when a man and a woman of similar faith, similar values, similar goals and similar judgment come together in marriage. Instead of two working as individuals, the pair works together. The work goes much more smoothly, progress appears more quickly, moments of weakness are compensated for and worked through. And after a lifetime together, they can look back and see a legacy of service that has stood as an example for many others over the years, and (Lord willing) will continue to so stand in the hearts and minds of those who have followed after them as they followed Christ.

Partners need not be mirror images; in fact, it can be helpful if they are not. If the man is strong in one area, the woman will be strong in another. Each values the other's strengths and is patient in the other's weaknesses. One is not more important than the other any more than the yolk of an egg is more important than the white. Both have their place, and both places are equally marvelous.

The concept of partnership is not in conflict with the concept of roles. Work is assigned in virtually every association of humans—each according to the skills and experience of the individual in question, normally. Such is the case with the association of marriage, except it is God who assigns the roles. Sociologists may bicker about the psychological and physiological differences between the sexes, but most of us acknowledge that men and women each tend to have certain strengths and weaknesses. The nurturing, emotive character that tends to be stronger in women suits them well in the role of mother and homemaker that God has given them (1 Timothy 2:15, Titus 2: 5). The physical strength, courage and aggression that tends to be stronger in men lends itself to leadership. Obviously there is a great deal of overlap in these character traits. It is equally obvious that the two halves complement each other well when they combine to make a whole. The wisdom of God is a marvelous thing.

A Story From The Office

"You are amazing in the kitchen, Wendy," Pia said, as she helped Wendy clear away the dinner dishes and serve dessert. Pia and Abel were in the process of acquiring

Abel and Pia
· Ages: He's 28, she's 28
· Married: 6 years
· Occupations: He's a landscaper, she's a homemaker and homeschool mom
· Children: 5 year old boy, Gabriel
Problem: Taking and giving criticism

Peter and Wendy's addiction to Alfred Hitchcock films. Previous installments in the monthly series had included *Dial "M" for Murder, North by Northwest, and Vertigo; Strangers on a Train* was about to join the list, as they ventured into the realm of black and white. Little Gabriel was providing an excuse for Claire to watch *Tangled* yet again.

"Well, I'll take credit for the apple dumplings," Wendy said, "but Peter did the burgers on the grill yesterday. I just heated them up."

Pia smiled a bit, crossed her arms, and glared at Abel. "A man who helps with the kitchen. How interesting."

"Don't get started," Abel said, mimicking Pia's half-smile and shaking his index finger.

"No, I would be interested in getting another perspective on this. Peter, I know you preached the other week about not talking bad about your husband or wife. But Abel doesn't think this is a problem at all, so I don't see how he can call it 'talking bad.'"

"OK," Peter said, not knowing quite where this was going.

"Abel refuses to do any housework. Refuses. He says that's my job. If we are going to have company and I'm running behind, he may vacuum. But he'll complain about it the whole time, and for a day afterward."

"I don't get any help from you at my job," Abel responded. "And it's as stressful and time-consuming as yours is. The last thing in the world I want to do after a long day of work is help you do your work. And don't start in again with how time-consuming the homeschooling thing is. That was your idea, not mine."

"But you liked the idea. Until the house started to suffer. I don't complain when you don't cut the grass or pay the bills quickly enough."

"Of course you do! All the time!"

Peter raised a hand. "All right, before the smiles start dropping off people's faces, let's dial this back a notch."

Unvoiced concerns: Abel and Pia did not communicate very well before marriage about their expectations of one another, and their incorrect assumptions may lead to long-term discontentment.

What Did Peter Tell Abel And Pia?

☐ Abel, Pia's right. A loving, supportive husband will want to reach out to support his wife. She loves you. She knows this is a burden for you. You can trust her not to abuse your helpfulness.

☐ Pia, Abel's right. He's the head of the household. Every time you question his judgment, he becomes less secure in that role; it may cause him to lash out. If you make a policy of just doing your job as well as you can, I promise you he will be less reactive if you ask for a bit of help once in a while.

☐ Wendy and I were just like you two once. Believe me, not only will you work through this, you will one day look back on it and laugh. Now finish your dessert; it's movie time.

A Story From The Bible

Aquila and Prisca (or Priscilla) are mentioned six times in the New Testament—always to-gether, never separately. They come on the scene in Acts 18 as Jewish emigrants from Rome, evidently already Christians, who supported Paul's work in Corinth by bringing him into their tent-making business. They traveled with Paul when he left for Jerusalem, staying behind in Ephesus and, evidently, playing a critical role in the birth of the church there. While there they taught Apollos more about the gospel of Jesus and encouraged him to take the truth to Achaia (Acts 18:24-28), where he followed up on Paul's good work (1 Corinthians 3:5-6).

The pair are mentioned prominently in Paul's letters as well. He sends greetings from the couple back to Corinth from Ephesus, probably near the beginning of his third preaching tour (1 Corinthians 16:19). By the time Paul wrote Romans, Aquila and Prisca had made it back to Rome and were serving the Lord and the church there (Romans 16:3-5). And at the end of Paul's life, he wrote from Rome back to Timothy in Ephesus, where he was being assisted by his favorite married couple (2 Timothy 4:19).

Perhaps it is significant that the makers of temporary dwellings moved about the world so frequently. Never seeming to grow deep roots anywhere, they went where their business (or perhaps the Spirit) took them. And wherever they landed, however long they stayed there, they worked for the Lord. There is little doubt that Paul's mind was eased consider-ably when he left Ephesus so quickly the first time, knowing he was leaving behind two of his best co-workers. And his confidence was justified when he returned a few years later to an established work that quickly acquired the reputation as a defender of the truth and a hub for evangelism in Asia. Aquila and Prisca's own propensity to teach others contributed considerably, no doubt, to the evangelistic fervor in Ephesus. The language appears to indicate that the couple cooperated in the teaching of Apollos (Acts 18:26).

The church "in their house" is noted in Romans 16:5 and 1 Corinthians 16:19. Scholars are divided over whether this means Christians gathered in their home on a regular basis, or that Christians simply lived with them as Paul likely had (children, relatives, servants, or other tenants). In either case, it is a clear indication that Aquila and Prisca did far more for the church than simply show up to take the Lord's Supper on the first day of the week. Their fellow Christians were an integral part of their everyday lives. Those closest to them tended to be Christians, and Christians tended to be those closest to them.

1. Can a woman participate in the teaching of a man? If so, how is it to be done within the constraints of God's roles for men and women? _____

   _____

   _____

2. How can Christians put the concept of "the church in their house" to work today? ____

   _____

   _____

What Did Peter Tell Abel And Pia?

☑ **Abel, Pia's right. A loving, supportive husband will want to reach out to support his wife. She loves you. She knows this is a burden for you. You can trust her not to abuse your helpfulness.**

☑ **Pia, Abel's right. He's the head of the household. Every time you question his judgment, he becomes less secure in that role; it may cause him to lash out. If you make a policy of just doing your job as well as you can, I promise you he will be less reactive if you ask for a bit of help once in a while.**

☐ Wendy and I were just like you two once. Believe me, not only will you work through this, you will one day look back on it and laugh. Now finish your dessert; it's movie time.

Strictly speaking, Peter said the first comment privately to Abel; Wendy said the second one privately to Pia. This is a classic case of neither party "winning" an argument, but both losing.

The tendency is always to want to help your spouse do a better job rather than working on yourself. After all, if my spouse fixed his/her problem, my "problem" would be a moot point. But if the wife respects her husband, she has to learn to accept His leadership, whatever form it takes. And if the husband loves his wife, he has to lead in such a way as to be a blessing to her and not a trial.

Lesson 6a

Two Are Better Than One

The Power Of Spiritual Fellowship

Jesus sent the seventy out in pairs (Luke 10:1). The apostles appear to have "paired up" in the early days of the church (Acts 1:13, 3:1). Paul almost always traveled with at least one preaching partner, and frequently more than one. Why exactly this custom was so prevalent among saints in the First Century, whereas preaching tandems such as Haggai and Zechariah (Ezra 5:1) are relatively rare in the Old Testament, is unclear. Perhaps there is something inherently unsettling in going "into all the world" (Mark 16:15) as opposed to going almost exclusively to the people of God. In any case, it is certain that partnership lent a needed and appreciated hand of support to workers in the kingdom then—and it is equally certain that Christians today need and receive the same benefit.

Ecclesiastes 4:9-12 reads, "Two are better than one because they have a good return for their labor. For if either of them falls, the one will lift up his companion. But woe to the one who falls when there is not another to lift him up. Furthermore, if two lie down together they will keep warm, but how can one be warm alone? And if one can overpower him who is alone, two can resist him. A cord of three strands is not quickly torn apart." If two people partnered together each want to be strong but only one actually feels strong in the moment, the courage and faith exhibited in the latter will bolster the former and rekindle the fire within. This only works, however, if each partner is rooted in the truth; a faithful person partnered with a faithless one will more likely destroy both than invigorate both (2 Corinthians 6:14).

God said from the beginning, "It is not good for the man to be alone" (Genesis 2:18). Thanks be to Him that He saw fit to give us aid in our walk with Christ just as He did for our walk through life.

A Story From The Congregation

Allen, Patience and their two children were regular visitors—when they were regular, anyway. They would attend every Sunday morning worship service for two months on end, and then the brethren would not see them for six months. Peter and Wendy were pretty sure they were not abandoning the Lord during the intervening months; they were just worshiping somewhere else. The church would have been glad to have Allen and the family as members, naturally, but they did not seem to want to be tied down. In fact, in three years of on-again, off-again visits, Allen and Patience had not given out so much as an address or phone number.

The subject of congregational loyalty and membership came up from time to time. No one wanted to pressure them or imply they were "better" than any other church in driving distance. At the same time, they knew the church had more to offer Allen and Patience than they were permitting—and that Allen and Patience almost certainly had more to offer the church.

Peter bumped into Allen in the home improvement store one morning, and stopped to chat for a few minutes in the plumbing aisle. When asked, Allen confirmed everyone's thinking—the family just made a habit of drifting from place to place, not making any firm attachments to a particular church.

"Why is that?" Peter asked. "Personally, I don't know what I would do without my brethren."

"I just think congregations miss the whole point of being a Christian," Allen replied. "I mean, 'the church' is just people, right? People in a location. Well, I'm people. I'm in a location. Why do I need to make it more complicated than that?"

"But you need fellowship," Peter countered. "You need oversight. You need peers looking out for your best interest, picking you up when you are down, joining forces with you in our common struggle."

"No, you need that. And that's fine. But I don't. I'm glad to be your brother in Christ and take His Supper with you. But other than that, I don't see the benefit."

What Did Peter Tell Allen?

☐ Are you sure you are speaking for your whole family? Your kids could use a peer group. Maybe your wife could as well. They may not be as comfortable in their relationship with Jesus as you are.

☐ That's a bit selfish, if you don't mind me saying so. Since when are your needs the only consideration? If you are really that strong, you have brothers and sisters in Christ who need you desperately.

☐ We can't pretend indefinitely that your "member-at-large" status is right with God. The elders won't want you to "just visit" with no intention of being a part of the work. If you have no intention of ever placing membership, you should probably "just visit" somewhere else.

A Story From The Bible

When the early church began to incorporate Gentile converts—starting with Cornelius and his family in Acts 10 and eventually leading to a fully heterogeneous Antioch fellowship in Acts 11—conflict was inevitable. The two groups had traditionally been at odds with one another, and even (for the Jews) seen their animosity as an inherently good thing. Now, with preachers like Paul preaching, "There is neither Jew nor Greek...for you are all one in Christ Jesus" (Galatians 3:28), change was coming. And people often respond poorly to change.

It became necessary for inspired preachers and prophets in all "factions" of the church to meet and compare messages; Acts 15 records the essentials of that meeting. They confirmed what we would have guessed—the Holy Spirit is not going to guide certain ones into one gospel and others into a different, conflicting one. When James, Peter and John extended "the right hand of fellowship" to Paul and Barnabas (Galatians 2:9), they were acknowledging their unanimity in the gospel of Jesus Christ, although that gospel was taking one group toward one group of people and the other group to another group.

The reconciliation of Jews and Gentiles fulfilled a host of Old Testament prophecies. Isaiah wrote of the Messianic era in Isaiah 11, noting in verse 6, "And the wolf will dwell with the lamb, and the leopard will lie down with the young goat, and the calf and the young lion and the fatling together, and a little boy will led them." This does not speak of some yet-to-be-fulfilled Messianic kingdom on earth, but rather the kingdom that exists now (Colossians 1:13). In the beginning, before death was brought into the world, all animals were vegetarians (Genesis 1:30). Wolves and lambs are not estranged from creation; they became estranged because of sin. Jesus rectifies the animosity that had grown up between human factions and brings us together into a harmonious whole, as had been the plan from the beginning.

Unfortunately, conflict sometimes arises anyway. Ironically, the same chapter that describes the coming together of the Jewish and Gentile elements of the church also describes a sharp disagreement and falling out between two brethren—not brethren who were from "opposite sides of the aisle," as it were, but rather long-time partners. Paul wanted to retrace the steps he and Barnabas had made during their first preaching tour. Barnabas agreed but wanted to take his cousin, John Mark, "who had deserted them in Pamphylia and had not gone with them to the work" (Acts 15:38). Their disagreement was so deep and irreconcilable that they permanently severed their partnership. But there is no reason to believe they did so with poor feelings toward one another; sometimes, through no specific fault of anyone, brethren work more effectively separately than they do together. The important thing is that both parties love the Lord, love one another, and remain committed to their common task. This they did. Paul even reconciled with Mark later, calling him "useful to me for service" (2 Timothy 4:11).

Relationships in the Lord will never be perfect; frequently they will be dysfunctional. We should always have cordial relations at least with brethren; if we cannot manage at least that, it speaks volumes about the relationship one or both parties have with Jesus. After all, fellowship with other Christians naturally results from a common fellowship with Jesus (1 John 1:3). And we should always strive to grow closer. But even if a connection with a particular brother or sister in Christ is less than it could be or should be, we can "preserve the unity of the Spirit in the bond of peace" (Ephesians 4:3).

1. List some other Old Testament prophecies that refer to the inclusion of Gentiles. (If you search for "Gentiles" in a concordance, be aware some versions use words like "nations" or "coastlands" instead.) _____
   _____
   _____

2. What should be the behavior of one Christian toward a brother who gives no indication of a desire to build a relationship? _____

_____

_____

in one's own life. Such an attitude hardly seems in harmony with the Biblical mandates for us to love our brethren and bear one another's burdens.

What Did Peter Tell Allen?

☐ Are you sure you are speaking for your whole family? Your kids could use a peer group. Maybe your wife could as well. They may not be as comfortable in their relationship with Jesus as you are.

☑ **That's a bit selfish, if you don't mind me saying so. Since when are your needs the only consideration? If you are really that strong, you have brothers and sisters in Christ who need you desperately.**

☐ We can't pretend indefinitely that your "member-at-large" status is right with God. The elders won't want you to "just visit" with no intention of being a part of the work. If you have no intention of ever placing membership, you should probably "just visit" somewhere else.

I cannot imagine a situation where I would rather have someone, anyone, stay away from worship services than participate. Surely it is better to have a brother in Christ maintain half a relationship with us than maintain none at all.

It's not our place to tell a brother in Christ how to conduct his family affairs, other than to point him toward the Scriptures. But the Scriptures do say that we should put our brethren's needs ahead of our own. Cutting oneself off from a congregation is sometimes a genuine issue of conviction. Most of the time, though, it has the appearance of simply not wanting to be involved in others' lives—or, more to the point, not wanting to have them involved in one's own life. Such an attitude hardly seems in harmony with the Biblical mandates for us to love our brethren and bear one another's burdens.

Lesson 7

...Or For Worse

| Finding Success In The Midst Of Failure |

Some Christians have bad marriages. Some Christians even get divorces. It's an ugly reality, but a reality nonetheless. As with every other command, the requirement of Matthew 19:6 is ignored from time to time. And saints are left in sin's wake, trying to overcome its ravages. Sometimes it means an innocent party trying to put the pieces back together, either in a second marriage or alone. Sometimes it means a guilty party coming to grips with a failure that will haunt him for a lifetime. Sometimes it means children splitting time between Mommy and Daddy who, for some unknown reason, don't live together anymore. And sometimes, tragically, it means faith being compromised, shattered or abandoned.

One of the most inspiring sights in the church is that of Christians determining, week after week, that a horrendous mistake (either theirs or another's) will not define them—that they will endure adversity, learn from the past, and serve as life lessons for their neighbors. What they absolutely refuse to do, on the other hand, is to use a disappointment in their most cherished earthly relationship break down a spiritual relationship with their Lord that is even more cherished. After all, we did not enter into a relationship with Jesus Christ because He promised us we would achieve or maintain carnal things; why then should we waver in our faith when things external to our faith become less satisfactory than we would wish them to be?

Jesus says in Matthew 10:37-38, "He who loves father or mother more than Me is not worthy of Me; and he who loves son or daughter more than Me is not worthy of Me. And he who does not take up his cross and follow after Me is not worthy of Me." True, the husband/wife relationship is not specifically mentioned. But if a failed marriage proves to be the "cross" we are asked to bear in His name, who are we to say it is too heavy?

A Story From The Office

Seeing Jake at church services was a rarity. Whitney said he considered himself a Christian and had been a member of a prominent church back in their hometown, but that he had not attended there since they were in high school—and not often even back then. "He's just never been that interested in spiritual things," she said.

Jake and Whitney
· Ages: He's 25, she's 26
· Married: 3 years
· Occupations: He's a graphic artist, she's a paralegal
· Children: 2 year old girl, Jada
Problem: Different faiths

After dating their senior year in high school and throughout college, they got married the weekend after their graduation. A job opportunity for Jake brought them to town a couple of months after that, and Jada followed soon afterward. Everything about Whitney's life had changed except her faith. She was hoping their new start would get Jake to take a new look at his relationship with Jesus. Instead he seemed more distant than ever. When he attended, he sat next to her with his arms crossed, scowling, willing to socialize with other families but resistant to forming any real friendships. He certainly did not want to study the Bible with Peter or the elders.

"He loves me, I know that," Whitney said to Wendy one Sunday. "And I love him. But he just doesn't want what I want out of life. He never has. And I'm starting to worry that he never will." Wendy suggested she make one more attempt to get Jake to come over to the house for dinner. When the appointed evening arrived and Wendy opened the door, it was just Whitney and Jada. No Jake. And Whitney was barely holding it together. Apparently, Jake had not only refused to come but had cursed at her, in front of Jada, on his way out the door to meet his friends at the sports bar.

"He's never been like this before" she said after Jada was fed and sequestered. He's not exactly been supportive, I know, but he's never given me the impression he thought I was wrong. He certainly has never talked to me like that before."

Peter and Wendy couldn't say much but what Whitney had already heard from others, and told herself, a hundred times—like how a relationship with Jesus helps us find a way to cope with difficult circumstances but not always erase them. Needless to say, they were not very effective at lifting her spirits.

"I can't imagine loving him more than I do," she said. "But the strain is really getting to me. And I just know he is going to want to keep Jada from being baptized when the time comes."

Unvoiced concerns: Jake had no real regard for Whitney's feelings or faith, and would interfere with her participation in the church more and more as time passed.

What Did Peter And Wendy Tell Whitney?

☐ Clearly your marriage is interfering with your faith. If you are really putting Jesus first, it might be time to start thinking about a divorce.

☐ All you can do is be the best Christian, wife and mother you can be. And you're doing that now. Stay strong. Do not grow weary in well-doing. It's not your job to save him; it's his job to save himself.

☐ Make Jesus an even bigger part of your marriage. Tell him, for instance, you have to talk about the Bible at least once a day—dinnertime would be ideal. Pray with Jada in his presence. Switch the music in the car to a Christian station. Every little bit of exposure to Jesus helps.

A Story From The Bible

Job's story provides perhaps more insight into the process of trials than any other book. Exactly how typical the exchange between Satan and God over the soul of Job was, we have no way of knowing; nor can we say definitively whether this sort of discussion still occurs in spiritual realms. But it is safe to say, however perfectly we fit into Job's situation, that the devil is active in quest of our souls—"a roaring lion, seeking someone to devour" (1 Peter 5:8). His "flaming arrows" (Ephesians 6:16) are ever flying at us, and we will be hurt badly by them if we are poorly armed against them.

Because Job's faith was genuine, because he was willing to serve God even if he received nothing for it in this life, he was able to endure on the day he did, in fact, receive nothing for it. All of God's blessings of wealth and family were stripped from him. But perhaps the worst trial did not come in the form of something Satan took, but rather what he left behind.

We forget, Job's wife was tempted as well. She lost just as many children as her husband, just as many possessions. And when her husband's health failed, she appears to have lost her faith as well. Job 2:9 reads, "Then his wife said to him, 'Do you still hold fast your integrity? Curse God and die!'" Not exactly the sort of encouragement Job needed at the lowest point of his life. It seems Satan knew having an unsupportive wife would be more of a trial to Job than having no wife at all. Why else would he leave her and take everything else?

But the very integrity his wife insulted was what kept Job stable. He was a servant of God, through and through. Surely he would rather have served God in favorable circumstances; who wouldn't? But he had confidence that God was still in control of his life, and that He would set things right in the end; as he said in Job 19:25 "As for me, I know that my Redeemer lives, and at the last He will take His stand on the earth."

James 5 uses the Job story to lift us up in our times of struggle—"You have heard of the endurance of Job and have seen the outcome of the Lord's dealings, that the Lord is full of compassion and is merciful." This should give us direction and encouragement when we do not get the support from our spouse that we think we need. The last thing in the world we want in a time of personal crisis is to be forced to bolster the faith of a spouse for fear that we may lose them as well. Ideally both parties would be able to come together and help one another through times of difficulty, and in so doing strengthen the marriage. Tragically, often the opposite is true; blame is passed around, regrettable things are said, and a bad situation becomes worse.

A faithless spouse can be a terrible burden for a Christian to bear. But God will give us the strength. It may be that our continued good behavior can bring the faithless one back from the brink; such seems to be the case for Job, as he and his wife stayed together and went on to have ten more children (Job 42:13-16). In any case, we should not allow the worst events of our life to push us toward an even worse tragedy.

1. Is there a Bible example of someone who did not have faith in God or in Jesus being compelled to submit to God's marriage law? If so, what implications does that have for non-Christians and their marriages? _____
_____
_____

2. Can one spouse lean so heavily on the other that it becomes a problem? Does the burden we are to bear for one another (Galatians 6:2) have limits? Explain your answer. _____
_____
_____

What Did Peter And Wendy Tell Whitney?

☐ Clearly your marriage is interfering with your faith. If you are really putting Jesus first, it might be time to start thinking about a divorce.

☑ **All you can do is be the best Christian, wife and mother you can be. And you're doing that now. Stay strong. Do not grow weary in well-doing. It's not your job to save him; it's his job to save himself.**

☐ Make Jesus an even bigger part of your marriage. Tell him, for instance, you have to talk about the Bible at least once a day—dinnertime would be ideal. Pray with Jada in his presence. Switch the music in the car to a Christian station. Every little bit of exposure to Jesus helps.

One of the toughest things for a Christian to do is allow someone, especially someone she loves, to fail. But ultimately, only Jake can make decisions for Jake. Questioning and undermining his role as the spiritual leader in the house would only put her confidence for his ultimate salvation in her words, not God's. A lack of regard for the teachings of 1 Peter 3:1-2 is a bad example, and it may very well turn into a bad habit. A lack of regard for Matthew 19:6 may be next.

Clearly, a Christian's first responsibility is to the Lord. Sometimes, not all the time, a Christian may not be able to serve the interests of her spouse and her Lord. With study and prayer, she will know when and if that time comes.

Lesson 7a

Weep With Those Who Weep

The Healing Power Of Fellowship

We live for heaven. We look to heaven. We prepare for heaven. But we do all of that on the earth. And the earth is full of hardships, trials and pain. We suffer in this earthly body daily, "longing to be clothed with our dwelling from heaven" (2 Corinthians 5:3). And at times, we suffer more. We have days that seem to never end, days when pain piles upon pain, when we almost despair of ever smiling again.

It may be in these dark days that brethren in Christ are the most important. "A friend who sticks closer than a brother" (Proverbs 18:24) need not be a fellow Christian necessarily, but only one who shares a faith in Jesus and in a heavenly rest from the woes of this life can truly help another Christian see God's light at the end of the long, dark tunnel. It is our responsibility as brothers and sisters in Christ to offer consolation to a fellow Christian who is in pain—both to ease their burdens in the moment as best we can, and to help make sure they maintain their greater long-term vision on heavenly things.

Showing sympathy is a tricky thing. The emotions of the one suffering, obviously, are rubbed raw. Often consumed utterly by their own woes, they are indifferent to the way they come across to others. As a result, they often appear to be rude, insensitive, self-involved, and generally unfriendly. We are all accountable for our behavior, even during times of stress. But loving, considerate brethren will see this sort of behavior and dismiss it quickly. "He didn't mean it like that," "That's not how she really feels," "That's just the anger and hurt talking," etc., should be phrases at the tip of our tongue when dealing with brethren in times of trial. If love "bears all things" (1 Corinthians 13:7), surely it will bear some hurt feelings in the context of intense grief and sorrow.

Knowing what to say, or whether to say anything at all, is not always easy. But simply "speaking from the heart" or "saying what I would want to hear" may not be the best thing—and surely we want to offer our best. Different people will respond differently to various approaches, depending largely on the existing relationship they have to the one offering comfort. A near-stranger taking the opportunity to "connect" is likely to be received poorly. "Relating" to one suffering by sharing similar experiences from your own life (which almost certainly are not really similar at all) will likely be taken as an attempt to make it "all about you." If you get the impression someone is trying to avoid you, they probably are; do not take it personally. Just pray for them and make your sympathy known in less direct ways such as a letter, text or private (emphasize private) Facebook message.

A Story From The Congregation

Matt and Mia were so happy when they brought little Levi home. They had tried for years to have a baby and had all but given up. Mia was bedridden for four months during the pregnancy. She went into labor six weeks early and stayed with Levi in the hospital for an extra week as he recovered from jaundice and low birth weight. But when the happy family finally arrived together at church services two months later, all of the stress was gone. Levi was the most beautiful baby boy any of us had ever seen. Matt and Mia were the happiest parents.

And just like that, he was gone. Bacterial meningitis. He went to the emergency room six months to the day after he was born, and he never came home. Peter officiated at a small, private service at the graveside. Mia did not look up the entire time; she just sat there, head in hands, sobbing. Matt just stared blankly into space. He looked like he had aged ten years.

They missed services the next week. They were on the back row the Sunday morning after that; they came in late and left during the invitation song. They made it through to the final prayer during the service that evening, though—barely. Peter shook Matt's hand as they headed for the door and the parking lot; clearly they were not in the mood to linger. He walked them out, not wanting to slow them down or force them into a social situation they were not ready for. "We just can't handle the crowd in the foyer yet," Matt said, as Mia hurried into the passenger seat of their car. "We'll get there. But right now it's too soon."

What Did Peter Tell Matt And Mia?

☐ We love you, and we're praying for you. Let us know if there's anything at all we can do.

☐ I know just how you feel. We went through this with Wendy's mom a few years ago. It's tough, but you will make it just like we did. Just keep leaning on the Lord; He will see you through.

☐ It's tough, I know, but you need to find a way to let your brethren in. Find someone and talk it out. It doesn't have to be me. But it has to be someone. Otherwise it will eat you up from the inside.

A Story From The Bible

Jesus waited two extra days in the territory beyond the Jordan River after He heard His friend Lazarus was deathly ill. Why did He do that? Instead of sharing the grief of Mary and Martha, why not spare them their grief instead? That was certainly what the sisters would have preferred. Both of them expressed complete and sincere confidence that He could have prevented his death (John 11:21, 32). And, of course, they were right; Jesus had healed any number of sick people during His ministry, many of them likely in the presence of Lazarus' family, many of them certainly as sick as he was. He even proved in healing the centurion's servant that He could exhibit His power without even being with the one who was sick (Luke 7:1-10); Jesus would not have had to go to Bethany at all.

Jesus certainly did not wait because He was indifferent to Lazarus' fate or his sisters' suffering. His love for Lazarus was unquestioned; word would not have been sent to Jesus had there not been knowledge that He would be moved by word of the illness. And once He arrived in Bethany, his tears surely eliminated any doubt of His emotions (John 11:33-36).

Jesus knew something the others did not. He knew Lazarus' death would serve a greater purpose. He knew that by allowing Lazarus to pass away and then raising him from the dead, He would provide a testimony that would spread throughout Judea. Lazarus, who was wealthy enough at least to have property large enough for a house and a private tomb, was likely known by everyone in Bethany, as well as many in nearby Jerusalem. And word of a four-day corpse coming back to life in a public setting could not possibly stay hidden. In fact, we are told specifically that many came to believe in Jesus because of this act, while others spread the news to His enemies, resulting in a heightened need in their minds to have Him killed (John 11:45-53).

It continues to serve the same purpose today. By reading the inspired account of Lazarus' resurrection, we have in ourselves a heightened sense of Jesus' power over death, which will ultimately result in our own deliverance from the tomb. Jesus said in John 11:25, "I am the resurrection and the life; he who believes in Me will live even if he dies, and everyone who lives and believes in Me shall never die. Do you believe this?" The question goes out to us—do we believe? Do we have confidence that the life He offers is eternal? That no depth of sin is beyond His power to reach and to save?

If we do, then we should receive great comfort from this story. Yes, Jesus could remove the situation that is causing us so much pain and sorrow. And no, it does not appear that He will do so—at least, not right away. And unlike Mary and Martha, we may never understand why in this life. But that does not mean Jesus is any less powerful or less caring than we believed Him to be. It may be that He is trying to work something in us that would not be possible any other way. If nothing else, "the testing of your faith produces endurance" (James 1:3).

When Paul writes in Romans 8:28, "And we know that God causes all things to work together for good to those who love God, to those who are called according to His purpose," he does not mean that it is "good" that we lose a parent, or a job, or a marriage. He means that the events of our lives are being woven together in spiritual realms to create "good" in us, bringing us to the place of faith where He wants us to be. Good and bad events, happy and sad events, blissful and painful events, He uses all of them to make us over into the image of His Son, as he mentions in the next verse. This is the blessing that comes to all of the ones who are called by the gospel out of the world. Everyone has to suffer while here on earth. But our suffering can mean something—if we will have enough faith to wait for Him to address our situation in the way He has planned.

1. What do we want from the Lord in times of emotional crisis? What should we want the most? _____
_____
_____

2. What do we say to the skeptic who scoffs at the idea that an all-loving, all-powerful Savior would allow His people to suffer the way they often do? _____

_____

_____

What Did Peter Tell Matt And Mia?

☑ **We love you, and we're praying for you. Let us know if there's anything at all we can do.**

☐ I know just how you feel. We went through this with Wendy's mom a few years ago. It's tough, but you will make it just like we did. Just keep leaning on the Lord; He will see you through.

☐ It's tough, I know, but you need to find a way to let your brethren in. Find someone and talk it out. It doesn't have to be me. But it has to be someone. Otherwise it will eat you up from the inside.

Brothers and sisters in Christ are an important part of the recovery process. But it is not the place of the one offering the sympathy to determine the time, place and form of the recovery. Different people grieve in different ways. Forcing them to do something that "worked for us" is likely to build resentment, not trust and connection.

Try to eliminate "I know just how you feel" from your conversations. How can one person possibly know "just how" another person feels? Our attempts to help someone in pain not feel alone frequently will be taken as efforts at minimizing their situation or "putting it in perspective." They don't need perspective—not in the heat of the moment, at least. The time may come eventually for a more direct approach to sympathy—if, for instance, a protracted pattern of absence and ignored phone calls develops. In the meantime, maybe what they require more than anything is time and space. Remember, it's about what they need, not what you "need" to offer them.

Lesson 8

The Object Of Our Affection

Finding Romantic Love In God's Place And God's Way

Romantic love is one of the great blessings from God in this life. Not everyone is privileged to have it. Those who are should cherish it. More than that, they should grow it. "The wife of your youth" (Proverbs 5:18-19) should provide satisfaction throughout life, and the husband should do the same for his wife.

Romantic love is not interchangeable with carnal lust. "The lust of the flesh" (1 John 2:16) tempts us to use the body God gave us in a purely selfish way, without regard for anyone else—let alone God. Paul in 1 Corinthians 6:18-20 calls our physical body "a temple of the Holy Spirit who is in you." This should be enough to discourage us from participating in fornication. Prostitution in Corinth was linked to the Aphrodite cult; worshiping Aphrodite was akin to indulging the flesh to the uttermost. This sort of "worship" is the exact opposite of what God wants for His people. He wants servants—His servants first, and the servants of others next. And if we cannot bring ourselves to serve our own spouses, what does that say about us?

Romantic love combines the thoughtfulness of the love we should have for all mankind, and particularly for fellow Christians (1 John 4:21) with the excitement that the people of the world crave. By seeking someone to love selflessly, and not just to give us love, we find far more than a release for our carnal urges (1 Corinthians 7:3). We find a true partner for life who will enhance our life in ways we cannot possibly anticipate. And the longer that life together lasts, the deeper the love grows, and the more satisfied both husband and wife become in their marriage.

A Story From The Office

Simon and Stephanie were the textbook "empty nesters." With both their children away at college, they were left to themselves for the first time in more than twenty years. And they were struggling. Stephanie had gone back to school to finish her degree years before, thinking she would be able to help with paying for college—and that she would need something to fill her days once the kids

Simon and Stephanie
- Ages: He's 52, she's 49
- Married: 24 years
- Occupations: He's an accountant, she's a nurse practitioner
- Children: 22 year old daughter, Meaghan; 19 year old son, Garrett
Problem: Fading affection

were grown. Now the college fund was full, as were her days. But their marriage looked more and more empty.

Simon was about ten years away from retirement. There had been conversation in earlier years about him transitioning into a work-from-home situation with flexible days and hours; they wanted to do a summer touring and photographing national parks, just the two of them. But Simon had not brought the subject up in years, and Stephanie was frankly fearful of it being raised again. Their evenings together consisted mostly of him watching television and her either sitting quietly with him or reading in another room. The prospect of being cornered in a car or hotel room with Simon for three consecutive months was unthinkable.

All this came out after a sermon one Sunday evening about making marriage work. Peter had suggested young couples should start planning for their lives after children in the same way as they do for their lives with children—lay a common foundation, and build on it constantly. When Wendy greeted Stephanie afterward in the foyer and asked about her kids, Stephanie started to well up with tears. Wendy pulled her aside, and Stephanie began describing her fears for her own marriage. Before too many details could come out, she told Claire to take the car and fend for herself for the evening, and the four of them went together for a sandwich.

Before he addressed Stephanie's concerns, Peter asked Simon what he thought of the sermon. He was surprised to hear him open up a bit, basically voicing the same sort of concerns Stephanie had shared with Wendy. "We were never the lovey-dovey types," Simon said. Then he looked over at Stephanie. "Well, I wasn't, anyway. She wanted me to call her pet names and things like that, which I thought was silly. I thought flowers on our anniversary and a nice gift on her birthday were enough." He was tearing up a bit. "I don't know. Maybe I was wrong."

"And I don't want to sound ungrateful," Stephanie said. "Simon is the best man I know. And the lovey-dovey stuff would have been nice, sure. But it's not the most important thing. I realize that now. Still, I didn't get married so I could have a good friend. And that's what we feel like sometimes to me. And maybe not even that."

Unspoken concern: Simon and Stephanie had blown their best chance of growing their relationship through years of neglect, and they might be stuck in their rut permanently.

What Did Peter And Wendy Tell Simon And Stephanie?

☐ Do the vacation. If work does not permit an entire summer off, settle for a couple of weeks. Isolate yourself from everything but each other. The love is still in there; you just have to find it and rekindle it.

☐ Shake up the weekly schedule. Go to new restaurants. Read books together and discuss them—even if it means just saying why you didn't like them. Learn some two-player card games. Try to create situations where conversation will be generated. Meaningless talk may grow into meaningful talk.

☐ Spend quality time around other couples. See what makes them work. Ask for advice if you are comfortable doing so.

A Story From The Bible

Every scholar seems to have a slightly different take on the Song of Solomon. Solomon is getting married; we can agree on that much. He dotes on his bride-to-be and finds her beautiful. But does she return his affection? Is the shepherd to whom she refers in Song of Solomon 1:7 and throughout the book a reference to Solomon himself, making it a beautiful and classic love story? Or is he someone else, her true love, to whom she is drawn even after her betrothal? The fact that she repeatedly calls her beloved a shepherd in her dreams, and the way Solomon is presented in all his majesty by the others in the book (Song of Solomon 3:6-11, for instance) moves me to think that this is a love triangle. Perhaps the Shulammite will go through with her marriage; but even if she does, her heart will remain with another. It is truly ironic. Solomon could have had virtually any woman he wanted—and he did have a thousand of them, according to 1 Kings 11:3. But the one for whom he has true, deep affection will never truly be his. She prefers the thought of cavorting in the pasture with a poor shepherd than living in the lap of luxury with the richest man in the world.

But even if we came to an agreement on the number of characters in the story, there is still plenty of room for disagreement with regard to the main point being put forward. It is much like reading poetry in other settings; the reader has a tendency to see in the text the point that he already believes, or that speaks to his or her specific situation in life, or that rationalizes a course of action already decided upon. Whether this is a poor way of reading poetry in a secular classroom can be debated. When it is Biblical, inspired poetry under consideration, the reader must make sure not to come to any conclusion that is negated by more literal and specific passages of Scripture. If the Bible all comes from God, we must believe it speaks in a single voice, without contradiction.

Perhaps the obvious explanation, especially being as surrounded as we are with Hollywood's idea of romantic love, is that Song of Solomon describes the pursuit of one's "soulmate." If the "shepherd" is Solomon, the bridge is simply being built between people of different cultures, ethnicities and economic backgrounds. Such relatively insignificant points pale in comparison to the connection that is made between a man and a woman who truly adore one another. If the Shulammite's true love is someone other than Solomon, the point is enhanced even more. She does not give her heart to a man simply because of the lifestyle he can provide. She wants to connect to her man on a deep emotional level that transcends matters of economics and comforts. (It is worth noting, however, that the book gives no indication that she actually rejects Solomon for her husband, although there is certainly room for the possibility that she would do so eventually.)

An almost diametrically opposed point to this one can be made as well. Perhaps the Shulammite is the villain in this story, not the hero. She has committed herself to marry Solomon, whatever the conditions (willing or not) may have been for her betrothal. He showers her with gifts, compliments and attention. Repeatedly he shows concern for her in her bedchamber, determined that no one should disturb her sleep. And while he protects her and provides for her, she is dreaming of someone else. And this "someone else" offers nothing of substance to her—only the thrill of the moment. And she rejects (in her dreams, at least) the security and provision offered by her husband in favor of a romp in the hay, literally, with him.

1. What is the biggest lesson you learn from a study of the Song of Solomon? _____

_____

_____

_____

2. How important is romantic love in a Christian marriage? Explain your answer. _____

_____

_____

_____

What Did Peter And Wendy Tell Simon And Stephanie?

☑ **Do the vacation. If work does not permit an entire summer off, settle for a couple of weeks. Isolate yourself from everything but each other. The love is still in there; you just have to find it and rekindle it.**

☑ **Shake up the weekly schedule. Go to new restaurants. Read books together and discuss them—even if it means just saying why you didn't like them. Learn some two-player card games. Try to create situations where conversation will be generated. Meaningless talk may grow into meaningful talk.**

☑ **Spend quality time around other couples. See what makes them work. Ask for advice if you are comfortable doing so.**

I don't flatter myself. A tidbit or two of advice from me is unlikely to reverse a trend of decades. It may wind up that unromantic couples may have to settle for being "safely" married rather than "happily" married. But there's no reason for them to assume they are incapable of more. The less satisfied they are in their marriage, the more likely they will look for satisfaction elsewhere.

Virtually any time spent together is a good idea, especially if a specific task is involved. I would not encourage a protracted car trip, as the potential for disaster is considerable. But virtually anything (within the bounds of propriety and godliness, of course) is better than lingering in the unsatisfying status quo.

Lesson 8a

Loving Him Who First Loved Us

Displaying A Loving Attitude Toward A Loving Lord

Jesus said, "If you love Me, you will keep My commandments" (John 14:15). And plenty of preachers, including this one, have leaned heavily on that verse to emphasize the importance of obedience in the life of a Christian. No one can call himself or herself a Christian while maintaining an indifferent attitude toward the will of Jesus.

Jesus did not say love and obedience are the same thing. He said they go hand in hand. One who loves Jesus will keep His commands. But mere obedience is no guarantee that we share the same love He showed to us. It is significant that, having any number of commands from which to choose, Jesus decided to sum up "the whole Law and the Prophets" by requiring God's people to love God and love each other (Matthew 22:34-39). Certainly our willingness to obey our Lord distinguishes us as His people. But our willingness to do so out of love distinguishes us as such even more.

Most readers, if they know anything at all about Biblical Greek, know the difference between phileo love and agapeo love. The first is emotional; the second is dispassionate, wishing for the betterment of another. Most "love" in the New Testament is the second, including the love God has for His people and they for Him; Jesus uses it in the abovementioned texts. But the difference can be overstated. God has phileo love for us as well—"But when the kindness of God our Savior and His love for mankind appeared, He saved us" (Titus 3:4). We have phileo love for Jesus—"If anyone does not love the Lord, he is to be accursed" (1 Corinthians 16:22). It is the phileo love under consideration in Matthew 10:37, where Jesus says, "He who loves father or mother more than Me is not worthy of Me; and he who loves son or daughter more than Me is not worthy of Me."

Certainly we should pursue the will of our Savior in our lives. But we should be emotionally invested as well. We have no trouble becoming emotional over the things of the world we enjoy—our friends, our entertainment, our sports, etc. Is it too much for Jesus to ask that we give Him our affection as well as our devotion? And what does it say about our discipleship when we find it difficult to do so?

A Story From The Congregation

You know that person at church who is always complaining about something? Never satisfied with anything? Well, Norris was that person times two. He was always sounding off about the weather, or the government, or the economy, or his health. And it wasn't like he was struggling mightily. Norris was a self-employed accountant. Business ebbed and flowed like most business does, but judging from his house, the car he leased, and other outward appearances, he seemed to be doing pretty well. And considering his great wife and family, you would think he would have cause to crack a smile from time to time. Not so much.

Being a rather upbeat person, Peter tried from time to time to lighten the mood in their conversations, which tended to be somewhat gloomy. Generally he could get Norris to admit his life wasn't all misery and heartache. But inevitably they would return to the subject of how his life's circumstances could not permit the kind of ongoing sense of joy Peter was always experiencing and extolling.

One day in particular got under Peter's skin. Norris was complaining in the foyer after services about a Christian brother (who worshiped with a different congregation) who had pulled his business and gone to a competitor. "He's trying to pinch pennies," Norris groused. "I told him this CPA he's going to gets results by skirting the law, that he was going to wind up paying a lot more in penalties than he's saving. But does he listen? No. Does he appreciate the service I've offered him for seven years? No. Does he support his brother in Christ who's trying to make an honest living? No."

"I could make a lot more money doing it the other way, you know. But I'm a dying breed; I believe in holding to the letter of the law, even if it costs my clients a little, even if it costs me my clients. The time is coming when I'm probably going to have to close up shop entirely. But hey, my relationship with Jesus comes first, right?"

What Did Peter Tell Norris?

☐ Well, that stinks. Hey, I see someone I need to talk to. Will you excuse me?

☐ You just have to have faith Jesus will work it out for you. I don't think for a minute that He'll let it get that bad. And to be candid, I bet it's not quite as bad as you are letting on even now.

☐ You don't get any extra credit from me for acting like a Christian ought to act. Sure, life in Jesus has its downside. But if you properly appreciate the upside, you don't mind the downside so much.

A Story From The Bible

I think we all wish we knew a little bit more about the way Jesus' discussion with Nicodemus went. We know that Nicodemus was intrigued enough by the things he had heard and seen that he visited the Lord by night, saying, "Rabbi, we know that You have come from God as a teacher; for no one can do these signs that You do unless God is with him" (John 3:2). We know he was perplexed by Jesus' assertion that he, a grown man, needed to be "born again" (John 3:3, 5). We know that Jesus' initial attempts to explain Himself only created further confusion in this man who thought he knew the Scriptures as well as anyone. We do not know how they left the discussion.

We do know a little bit. This man who would only visit Jesus by night stood up in Jesus' defense in John 7:50-51, when it appeared his colleagues in the Sanhedrin were ready to pass judgment on Jesus without due process: "Our Law does not judge a man unless it first hears from him and know what he is doing, does it?" he asked rhetorically, drawing ridicule instead of informed and honest discussion. Eventually, of course, the Sanhedrin did condemn Jesus to death in a mockery of a trial convened illegally in the middle of the night, but waiting to vote until sunrise to give the proceedings a veneer of respectability (Matthew 26:57-27:2); it is suggested by some that this approach was specifically designed to exclude ones such as Nicodemus and Joseph of Aramathea who might have been considered barriers to a quick and unanimous verdict.

In the end, Nicodemus' devotion to Jesus could not be hidden. Unable, it would seem, to do anything to stop the injustice heaped upon Jesus, Nicodemus brought a hundred pound of myrrh and aloes for His burial, which was to take place in Joseph's new tomb. Clearly such a gesture, done before the sunset that would begin the Sabbath, could not possibly have been missed; it almost certainly was made specifically in such a way so as to make it impossible to miss.

These three incidents in John's gospel chart the development of Nicodemus' commitment to Jesus. First he acknowledged His greatness as a teacher and prophet but apparently was unwilling to do so in public. Then he argued that Jesus should be treated fairly under the law against strong opposition from his peers, although there is no indication he actually argued for Jesus' innocence. Finally he made a significant and public gesture in support of Him, seemingly indifferent to the consequences that may arise.

At what point did Nicodemus become a disciple? That is for God to decide, not us. But surely if we want to consider ourselves a true follower of the Lord, we should be willing for people to know that such is the case. Beyond that, we should be willing to take a stand for Him in public. But even more so, a true disciple will care enough about the Lord to tend to His business, even at great cost of time, resources and/or reputation. Certainly such things are important to us, and we should not be embarrassed to admit as much. But the Lord means far more.

What kind of love do we have for the Lord? Is it a love that supports silently from the sidelines? Is it a love that speaks up only when extremes of deception and unfairness appear? Or is it a love that compels us to visible acts of support? If we are willing to sit idly by and watch Him blasphemed and mocked now, what makes us think we would have been any more supportive with Him at the cross? And if we condemn Nicodemus for hiding his faith early on, what does that say about us when we do essentially the same thing? If true faith and love move believers to take side with Him, regardless of consequences, then that is exactly what we should be willing to do.

1. What circumstances arise in which we are given opportunities to be noticeably on the side of Jesus, and at the same time opposed to most people around us? How do we respond? _____
_____
_____

2. Is there a situation in which being vocal in our support for Jesus can be a bad thing? Explain your answer? _____

_____

_____

One thing I would not do is offer some sort of assurance that the future will be brighter. Perhaps it will be, perhaps not. But the problem is not that life has given us too many lemons; it is that we have not yet found the right recipe for lemonade. Hanging our hopes on a changing climate is dangerous. It is far better to hope in Christ for strength to deal with problems than for relief from them.

What Did Peter Tell Norris?

☑ **Well, that stinks. Hey, I see someone I need to talk to. Will you excuse me?**

☐ You just have to have faith Jesus will work it out for you. I don't think for a minute that He'll let it get that bad. And to be candid, I bet it's not quite as bad as you are letting on even now.

☐ You don't get any extra credit from me for acting like a Christian ought to act. Sure, life in Jesus has its downside. But if you properly appreciate the upside, you don't mind the downside so much.

If instruction on priorities and values is what is needed, that is what should be supplied, with a healthy dose of sympathy and kindness. But that's not Norris' problem. Whiners will whine. If the conversation were more private, a heavier discussion about the joy or misery we make for ourselves might be appropriate. In a public setting, though, I suggest the "war of attrition" tactic — slowly wearing him down with positivity. That doesn't work for me very often, but at least I don't get dragged down into the complainer's emotional quagmire. I will offer support in my brother's trials; I do not offer to wallow with him in them.

One thing I would not do is offer some sort of assurance that the future will be brighter. Perhaps it will be, perhaps not. But the problem is not that life has given us too many lemons; it is that we have not yet found the right recipe for lemonade. Hanging our hopes on a changing climate is dangerous. It is far better to hope in Christ for strength to deal with problems than for relief from them.

Lesson 9

Purity First

Setting Yourself Up For Success

The easiest problem to solve is the one you never have to face. The best example of this may be infidelity. By avoiding circumstances that might compromise your marriage, celebrating the righteous pursuit of marriage in yourself and in others, and condemning the mockery our culture regularly makes of marriage, we can have every confidence that we can remain pure in an impure world.

Sensible people do not experiment with how much rat poison can be mixed into the meatloaf without causing serious health concerns. Yes, you can drive yourself crazy avoiding every conceivable circumstance that could lead to something—avoid pornography by shutting off your internet access, avoid people in immodest clothing by moving to Saudi Arabia, etc. Realistically, we are living in a sinful world, and we will have to associate with the sinful people in it to a certain degree (1 Corinthians 5:9-10).

Then again, Jesus did suggest gouging out your eye as a measure for avoiding hellfire (Matthew 5:29). Yes, He was probably exaggerating to make a point. But in the big picture, wouldn't it be worth it?

A Story From The Office

"Abstain from every form of evil" had been Peter's sermon theme that morning, based on 1 Thessalonians 5:22. In it he mentioned the policy he and Wendy had of not being alone with a member of the opposite sex. That afternoon they got a call from Diego, asking if they could meet with him and Bailey before evening services began. Turned out, Bailey had told Diego that afternoon that she had a standing "lunch date" between classes on Tuesday and Thursday on campus with a male friend, Todd, whom she had met in one of her classes.

"I just don't understand what the big deal is," Bailey said. "He's married, I'm married, it's completely platonic. Is it a sin to spend time with a man who isn't your husband?"

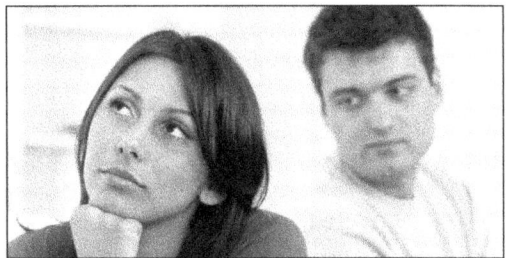

Diego and Bailey
- Ages: He's 26, she's 24
- Married: 2 years
- Occupations: He's a personal trainer, she's a student
- Children: None
  Problem: Other relationships with the opposite sex

"It's not a matter of it being a sin," Wendy said. "It's like Peter was saying this morning, we do little things every day to keep problems from coming up in the first place. It protects your marriage, it protects the other man's marriage, it keeps people from getting the wrong idea and thinking about you in a bad light. And let's be honest; plenty of affairs have started because of 'innocent' lunch dates. We've all seen it happen."

"I just don't like the idea that he doesn't trust me," Bailey argued.

"I do trust you," Diego replied. "But I'm not going to lie, it drives me crazy to think of you with another man. I would have put a stop to this earlier if I had known."

Bailey turned and glared at him. "Don't you think you're being a bit hypocritical here?"

"What are you talking about?" Diego said. Of course, Peter and Wendy knew exactly what she was talking about, having discussed it between themselves many times.

"You're around women all the time!" Bailey exclaimed. "Hot, sweaty women in tights and sports bras. At least Todd is covered up when we have lunch."

"That's my job! I'm a trainer! How am I supposed to tell my clients what to wear? I'd get fired if I even tried, and probably sued for sexual harassment on top of that. Plus, it's a huge gym. I'm never alone with any of them, even in private workouts."

"Still, it's a lot more likely to lead to something than my lunches with Todd. Are you telling me none of these women has ever come on to you?"

"Sure, it happens sometimes. And I say no. Once it got a bit more uncomfortable than that, and I got my manager to assign her to another trainer."

"I can't believe you never told me that! Why didn't you tell me?"

"Because I thought you might overreact! What was I thinking?"

Unvoiced concern: Bailey had long resented the time Diego spent with other women; one or both of them may allow their resentment to rationalize taking an extramarital relationship to another level.

What Did Peter Tell Diego And Bailey?

☐ Our rules work for us. You need to develop rules for you to help you be accountable to each other. If you love each other and don't keep secrets from each other, you should be OK.

☐ Bailey, a private conversation is very different from a business relationship. Diego is accountable to managers who want to avoid personal entanglements as much as he does. It's not ideal by any means, but it's workable.

☐ Sounds like apples and apples to me. A restaurant and a gym are both about as private as you want them to be. Bailey, I'd strongly advise you to quit the lunches. Diego, I'd strongly advise you to think about a career change.

A story from the Bible

The course of the nation of Israel changes in 2 Samuel 11. Most obviously, David met the woman who would become the mother of his heir, Solomon. And although Solomon certainly had his share of failures, the three books he contributed to the Scriptures more than balance that out in the big picture, at least as far as we are concerned today.

The rest of the ripples placed in the pond by the actions of David and Bathsheba were negative, even devastating. As Nathan prophesied in 2 Samuel 12:10, David was cursed to battle for his crown for the better part of the rest of his reign. Major insurrections forced David twice into temporary exile. One of those insurrections was stirred on by David's son, Absalom, who wound up being killed himself. Absalom's rebellion likely was a result of instability in David's family, which no doubt was exacerbated when a much younger half-brother was named the heir. This choice eventually led to another rebellion led by another half-brother, Adonijah, who himself was killed by Solomon (1 Kings 1-2).

This was all avoidable. Every bit of it.

It began with something simple: David, "at the time when kings go out to battle," stayed at home instead (2 Samuel 11:1). How many times do we get in trouble with the wrong thing simply because we were not busy enough in the right thing? Had David been properly engage with his responsibilities as king, he would not have been in position to entangle himself with Bathsheba.

Then David went up to his rooftop and saw Bathsheba bathing. We can waste as much time as we like apportioning blame here. Did David have reason to expect he would see her naked? Was it in fact his plan to do so? How much privacy did Bathsheba have a right to expect? How much did she want? The bottom line is, they both had opportunity to avoid the situation; only one of them acting would have been enough, and neither did.

David sent for her, and she came. Again, did Bathsheba know what the king wanted? Could she legally refuse his overtures? Had she, in fact, orchestrated the entire affair? The Bible does not lead us in one direction or the other, and that is likely with a purpose. Both acted; both were to blame. That's all we need to know.

When her pregnancy became known, David chose to hide his sin by disguising the consequences. But when noble Uriah refused to cooperate by going in to his wife, David felt he had no alternative but to arrange for Uriah's death, marry Bathsheba, and (presumably) pass the birth off as premature.

Making a good decision can avoid countless opportunities to make poor ones. Making a poor decision not only opens the door to more poor ones, it helps us rationalize them.

If we, like God, can have eyes that are "too pure to approve evil" (Habakkuk 1:13), we will have fewer occasions to wrestle with "ethical dilemmas" down the road.

1. Define "situation ethics." How does it relate to David and Bathsheba's progression of behavior? _____

_____

_____

2. How pervasive does lewdness need to be in an environment for us to shun that environment? _____

_____

_____

What Did Peter Tell Diego And Bailey?

☐ Our rules work for us. You need to develop rules for you to help you be accountable to each other. If you love each other and don't keep secrets from each other, you should be OK.

☐ Bailey, a private conversation is very different from a business relationship. Diego is accountable to managers who want to avoid personal entanglements as much as he does. It's not ideal by any means, but it's workable.

☑ **Sounds like apples and apples to me. A restaurant and a gym are both about as private as you want them to be. Bailey, I'd strongly advise you to quit the lunches. Diego, I'd strongly advise you to think about a career change.**

I really, really try to avoid giving advice—especially advice that requires someone to do something horribly difficult that I myself don't have to do. Changing jobs is at the top of the list. I cannot say it is sinful to work in an environment where immodest dress is common. But when it begins to directly impact your service to God or your marriage, you have to start thinking about priorities — especially if you are young enough to consider a career change.

Honesty, if not coupled with restraint, may not always be the best policy. Hearing about the many opportunities one's spouse had for infidelity and passed on can become burdensome. Before too long, resentment can set in, and you are back to choosing between full disclosure and peaceful relations.

Lesson 9a

The Cure For Cancer

Protecting The Body Of Christ From Itself

They say an ounce of prevention is worth a pound of cure. The logic is undeniable; it is easier to avoid a problem than to work one's way out of one. Such is the case for the church as surely as it is for the individual members of it. That is why church overseers are to be appointed who will "be able...to refute those who contradict" (Titus 1:9). On-the-job training can be disastrous; the church can have much more confidence in a man who has demonstrated a willingness to oppose error in principle than one who tries to avoid "sticky subjects" until they become real.

Admittedly, dealing with issues proactively can be tiresome to many brethren; they would rather dwell on matters that have more obvious implications for their current situations in life. And church leaders can get so proactive about "brotherhood issues" that they borrow trouble, creating controversies where none previously existed. Preachers can become so enamored of an in-depth consideration of "issues" that they neglect matters that bear directly on the salvation of souls; such ones "strain out a gnat and swallow a camel," to use Jesus' language from Matthew 23:24.

The best way for a church to be healthy is to be "constantly nourished on the words of the faith and of the sound doctrine" (1 Timothy 4:6). Sound doctrine will, by its nature, expose those who live contrary to God's moral and doctrinal laws (1 Timothy 1:8-11). But it does more than that. It provides spiritual grounding to the individual believers as well as a framework with which they can work together. The more we allow the "pure milk of the word" (1 Peter 2:2) to nourish us as individuals, and the closer we work together as brethren, the more that same word will empower us to be the body of Christ in the way we ought to be.

A Story From The Congregation

Right away, Peter and Wendy had a feeling Marvin was going to be difficult. That was fine; there are difficult brethren in pretty much every church. But when the church's eldership dissolved, it got considerably worse quickly. With both of his grown children out of service, and with a reputation as a bit of a hothead, Marvin knew he would never be appointed an elder himself. But he learned quickly that in business meetings, the loudest voice in the room tends to carry the day. And Marvin could be pretty loud when he wanted to be.

The first order of business was the re-establishment of the eldership. The church had several men who seemed, on the surface at least, to be worthy of consideration. So Peter volunteered to preach a few sermons on the work and character of congregational overseer. Almost immediately Marvin made it clear, in private comments and in the men's business meetings, that he had almost impossibly high standards for elders. Every line of 1 Timothy 3 and Titus 1 was scrutinized and studied from every conceivable angle. If someone didn't suit every member in every category, according to Marvin, he should be rejected.

Peter spoke up during one business meeting on the subject of standards. "Any church that says it wants perfect elders," Peter said, "is saying, in effect, it doesn't want elders at all. No Christian is going to be perfect. So naturally no elder candidate is going to be perfect."

"No one said elders had to be perfect," Marvin chimed in quickly. "But we have to follow the letter of the law. And if we can't get everyone to agree on what an elder should be, we should play it safe and wait until we can reach a consensus."

What Did Peter Tell Marvin?

☐ Forcing the majority to go along with the minority's judgment isn't any more scriptural than the reverse. Being of the same judgment doesn't mean believing exactly the same thing; it means agreeing to act in the same way, and trusting your brethren to be led by the word as you are being led.

☐ Every congregation needs elders. They won't be perfect in any case. We just need to find the men who measure up to the standard as closely as possible, install them, and trust that they will grow into the position.

☐ I think you are missing the forest for the trees. The descriptions in 1 Timothy 3 and Titus 1 give us a sketch of an elder, not a photograph. If we can read them and they remind us of a particular brother, he's likely someone who should be receiving serious consideration.

A Story From The Bible

The apostle John was the last of the apostles to pass from this life. Most scholars believe it was in the last decade of the First Century that he penned his epistles, each one emphasizing the importance of apostolic authority and condemning those who set themselves up as a law unto themselves. Jesus had required him and the other apostles to teach the next generation of disciples "to observe all that I commanded you" (Matthew 18:20); clearly, John was determined to do just that. And when someone put his own will ahead of or in place of the will of His Master, he condemned it in the strongest of tones (2 John 9).

Such a condemnation was required when he wrote to "the beloved Gaius" in 3 John. We do not know anything about the church of which Gaius was a part other than what John writes. But we have enough information to know about the two forces that were in conflict there.

One is seen in the character of a man named Demetrius. Verse 12 reads, "Demetrius has received a good testimony from everyone, and from the truth itself; and we add our testimony, and you know that our testimony is true." Jewish tradition required the testimony of two or three witnesses to corroborate a fact being placed in evidence (Deuteronomy 19:15, 2 Corinthians 13:1). Demetrius had testifying for him (one) popular opinion; (two) God's revelation, which likely came to Demetrius directly; and (three) John's own inspired, apostolic judgment. This should be plenty to convince someone who regards Divine truth that Demetrius is on the side of righteousness in the debate that was affecting that particular local church.

The same principle applies to us today as we ascertain which side, if any, of a dispute among brethren should receive our support. Romans 8:16 reads, "The Spirit Himself testifies with our spirit that we are children of God." Although we do not have direct inspiration as the church had in times past, we do have indirect inspiration. We can read the words given by the Spirit and use them as a spiritual measuring stick. If our lives "line up" with the word, that shows our godliness. The Spirit cannot testify on behalf of two parties who disagree on a doctrinal matter, since the Spirit speaks with a single voice. The truth is with the one who has "the Spirit who is from God, so that we may know the things freely given to us by God, which things we also speak, not in words taught by human wisdom, but in those taught by the Spirit, combining spiritual thought with spiritual words" (1 Corinthians 2:12-13).

The other side of the argument, the one guided by "words taught by human wisdom," is seen in Diotrephes. Also a partaker in the fellowship with Demetrius and Gaius, this man had a very different attitude. John wrote that he "loves to be first among them, does not accept what we say" (3 John 9). John does not consider this merely a personal affront; he sees the rejection of his Spirit-inspired words as a rejection of Jesus Christ Himself. It is not surprising that a prideful individual such as Diotrephes would go so far as to make an accusation against an apostle or set himself up as a one-man fellowship committee (3 John 10).

Between the descriptions of these two men, John writes in verse 11, "Beloved, do not imitate what is evil, but what is good." We need to decide for ourselves which of these two men is to be an example for us as we pursue godly fellowship with brothers and sisters in Christ within a local church. If we are led by the Spirit, as was Demetrius, we will accept anyone who stands for truth—not as we define it or as we apply it, but as God has revealed it. If we are led by a spirit of pride and self-exaltation, we will imitate Diotrephes, as this is the best way to make ourselves important among the brethren. But Diotrephes should stand warned: godly men and women will not stand for this sort of factious, self-serving behavior. Always we should correct with patience, but Paul writes in Titus 3:10-11, "Reject a factious man after a first and second warning, knowing that such a man is perverted and is sinning, being self-condemned."

1. What does it mean if two differing parties in the church both use Scripture to defend their position? _____
   _____
   _____
   _____

2. At what point does the church need to be more stringent in its correction of error? And how does it go about doing so? _____
   _____
   _____
   _____

What Did Peter Tell Marvin?

☑ **Forcing the majority to go along with the minority's judgment isn't any more scriptural than the reverse. Being of the same judgment doesn't mean believing exactly the same thing; it means agreeing to act in the same way, and trusting your brethren to be led by the word as you are being led.**

☐ Every congregation needs elders. They won't be perfect in any case. We just need to find the men who measure up to the standard as closely as possible, install them, and trust that they will grow into the position.

☑ **I think you are missing the forest for the trees. The descriptions in 1 Timothy 3 and Titus 1 give us a sketch of an elder, not a photograph. If we can read them and they remind us of a particular brother, he's likely someone who should be receiving serious consideration.**

Some Christians with naturally forceful personalities may take advantage of the absence of elders to press their will upon the majority. Whether it is done intentionally or not is not the only issue. Existing as a cohesive body requires each member to acknowledge the difference between his firmly held opinion and Divine revelation, and then to be willing to yield for the sake of peace and unity.

This is not the same as compromising truth. We can agree that, for instance, elder candidates should be in control of their households without agreeing completely on how that control should be demonstrated.

Forsaking All Others

Dealing With Infidelity, Before And After

Fidelity is defined as devotion, loyalty, allegiance. It is the willingness to be faithful in a commitment, despite changing circumstances. Infidelity, obviously, is the opposite. And it is no accident that it is used almost exclusively in the context of marriage in our culture. Marriage is the ultimate test of devotion in this life, and fornication the ultimate failure. Infidelity is a brutal blow to the relationship, and there may be no recovery from it.

If a husband and wife are to be "one flesh"—and this is true for no other relationship in the life of either one—then clearly they must be connected to one another in a far more intimate way than with any other person. Confidences should not be kept, and secrets absolutely should not be shared with others instead of one's spouse.

Making a practice of laying bare our souls before our spouses leaves us hopelessly compromised and vulnerable, not a position that we are likely to find comfortable. But it is only in that moment of pure honesty that we can be who we actually are, rather than what we want to be or what we want others to perceive us to be. The feeling of being absolutely truthful, even about our weaknesses and failures, creates a bond unlike any other.

But when we find it impossible to trust the one that we have come to trust the most, the pain is as intense as the honesty. That is why we must reserve our deepest intimacy for the one closest to us—and do everything in our power to be true to that one.

A Story From The Office

Everyone was shocked when Gabrielle stepped out into the aisle and walked up to the front pew. They were more shocked when they found out why. "It was a one-time thing with someone at work," she said. She and Howard were working it out. They wanted our prayers. They didn't seem to want to talk about it beyond that, and Peter and Wendy certainly didn't want to pry. Peter offered counseling, and they declined.

Six months later, Gabrielle was on their doorstep, sobbing. Howard had kicked

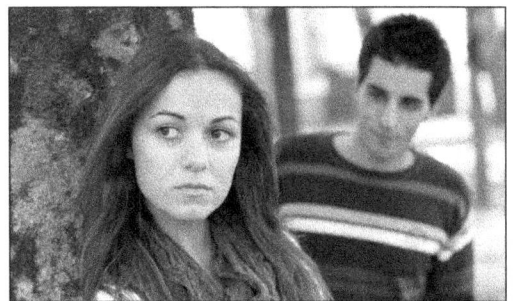

Howard and Gabrielle
- Ages: He's 30, she's 29
- Married: 4 years
- Occupations: He's a project manager, she's a loan counselor
- Children: None

Problem: Recovering from infidelity

her out of the house. As it turned out, she had been unable to find employment elsewhere, as she had said she would. Instead, she had accepted a promotion—a promotion that had her working closely with "him." Howard had tried to surprise her at lunch that day. He surprised them both.

Peter finally convinced Howard to come over, and the four of them sat down together. Gabrielle insisted that there was nothing going on between her and her coworker—or anyone else. Peter and Wendy believed her, and Howard seemed to as well. "But that's not the point," he insisted. "How am I supposed to trust you if you hide things?"

"I wasn't trying to hide anything," she responded. "I got the promotion a week ago. I didn't know I would be working with...him. I was trying to find a way to get around that before I broke the news to you."

After a couple of hours of back and forth, it boiled down to this: Gabrielle was not inclined to take a major step backward in her career and seriously deplete their finances just to avoid a situation that was already resolved; Howard was willing to take her back, provided she revived her search for another position and refused to spend any time with "him"—not even eating in the office cafeteria at the same time.

Unvoiced concern: The tension between the two of them was a long way from being resolved, and the marriage was in serious jeopardy.

What Did Peter And Wendy Tell Howard And Gabrielle?

☐ Gabrielle, your hesitation at breaking off contact with the other man is telling Howard you may still have feelings for him. If you value your marriage, you will do everything you can to cut off communication, up to and including quitting your job.

☐ Howard, you need to decide if you have forgiven her or not. If you have, you should trust her to behave in a proper way. That means normal association with all her coworkers. The more you call her commitment into question, the less commitment there is likely to be.

☐ Gabrielle, bring Howard up to the office one day for lunch. Dote on him. Make sure "he" sees. Put lots of new pictures of Howard on your desk. Make it obvious to everyone, especially Howard, that there is no competing with him for your affections.

A Story From The Bible

Ordinarily, being asked to play the part of God in an ongoing drama would have to be considered a tremendous compliment. But under the circumstances, I don't think Hosea saw it that way.

Giving herself to one man after another (and judging from the symbolism in Hosea 1:8-9, giving birth to a child by one of them), Gomer perfectly epitomized the faithless nation of Israel. Having accepted the blessings that came from a loving, nurturing God, Israel used those blessings to honor another: "For she does not know that it was I who gave her the grain, the new wine and the oil, and lavished on her silver and gold, which they used for Baal" (Hosea 2:8). Not properly embarrassed over her lewd behavior, having given herself to one false god after another, the one that should have been the holy spiritual bride of the God of heaven would instead be fully stripped of all blessings and dignity, thrown into the wilderness (Hosea 2:1-3).

Did Hosea know what kind of wife Gomer would make ahead of time? He is told to take "a wife of harlotry and have children of harlotry," according to Hosea 1:2, so it seems so. But that does not mean there was not legitimate love in Hosea's heart for his wife. Indeed, the symbolism works much better when we consider Hosea standing in the role of God, who loved His people from the beginning and was willing to be merciful to them in their faults and shortcomings for a time, but who eventually could not allow an unceasing pattern of betrayal to go unaddressed. And extending the metaphor to all humanity, God knew the need of mankind for a Savior before mankind ever was. Romans 8:28-30 indicates the predetermined plan of God to conform us to "the image of His Son"—not to trust that we would be perfect and then come up with a plan on the fly if we disappointed Him.

The message of reconciliation continues to come up in the story of God and His people. We see it even in Hosea. As angry and vengeful as God was, He still spoke of His beloved in tender tones, indicating His desire to bring her back to Him: "Therefore, behold, I will allure her, bring her into the wilderness and speak kindly to her. Then I will give her her vineyards from there, and the valley of Achor as a door of hope, and she will sing there as in the days of her youth, as in the day when she came up from the land of Egypt" (Hosea 2:14-15).

Terms would have to be set and respected for fellowship to be restored. He says in Hosea 3:3, "you shall stay with me for many days. You shall not play the harlot, nor shall you have a man; so I will also be toward you." His hope was that the nation, after chastening, would remember the blessings that came with a marriage to Him and would be moved to return to her first love.

But Hosea continued to love his bride. God urged him to take Gomer back despite her adultery (Hosea 3:1). Perhaps she also learned her lesson and remembered how good her life was with her true husband. We certainly hope so. Sometimes this is not possible with a marriage soiled by adultery, and Matthew 19:9 tells us through necessary inference that a wronged party should not be blamed for ending a marriage because of an unfaithful spouse, and perhaps even marrying again without blame. But surely the best-case scenario, the situation to be most sought after, is true repentance, true forgiveness, and true reconciliation.

1. Find other passages in which spiritual infidelity is likened to harlotry. Describe the similarity of a literal wife giving herself "mostly" to her husband, and Christians giving themselves "mostly" to Christ. _____

_____

_____

2. Is it appropriate for the "innocent" spouse to place terms upon the return of a wayward husband or wife? If so, explain what form those terms might take. _____

_____

_____

What Did Peter And Wendy Tell Howard And Gabrielle?

☑ **Gabrielle, your hesitation at breaking off contact with the other man is telling Howard you may still have feelings for him. If you value your marriage, you will do everything you can to cut off communication, up to and including quitting your job.**

☑ **Howard, you need to decide if you have forgiven her or not. If you have, you should trust her to behave in a proper way. That means normal association with all her coworkers. The more you call her commitment into question, the less commitment there is likely to be.**

☐ Gabrielle, bring Howard up to the office one day for lunch. Dote on him. Put lots of new pictures of Howard on your desk. Make it obvious to everyone, especially Howard, that there is no competing with him for your affections.

Forgiveness is one thing; pretending like a horrible thing never happened at all is quite another. Howard had every right to ask Gabrielle to do whatever it took to put his mind at ease, however unreasonable she may think it is.

Outward signs of affection are fine and good in a marriage. But an unchanged dynamic between Gabrielle and her coworkers was sure to make Howard's fears of another misstep continue and fester. And in my mind, anyway, it would not be unreasonable for him to respond that way.

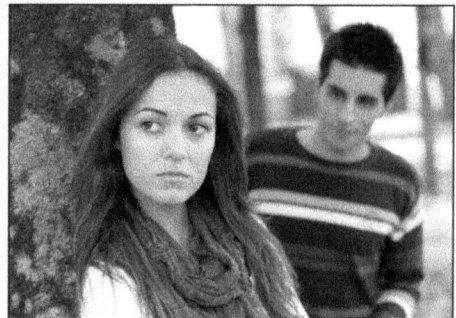

Lesson 10a

Following The Pattern

What To Imitate, And How To Imitate It

It is easy to spout platitudes such as, "Speak where the Bible speaks, be silent where the Bible is silent." It is somewhat more difficult to put those concepts into effect. The fact is, people across the spectrum of our brethren—indeed, the spectrum of our society—claim to be following the teachings of Jesus Christ; the cacophony of competing and contradictory voices in the modern religious forum tells us how inadequate that measuring stick is. The principle is excellent, but we need to find a way to effectively and consistently implement it.

Jesus Himself said, "Not everyone who says to Me, 'Lord, Lord,' will enter the kingdom of heaven, but he who does the will of My Father who is in heaven will enter" (Matthew 7:21). We know Jesus does not mean that only perfect law-keepers will be saved, since none of us qualifies on that front (1 John 1:8). No, He is speaking of a lifestyle choice rather than an unbroken pattern of behavior. Some are determined to fit their lifestyle into conformity with the will of God; others are determined to twist the Scriptures to accommodate their lifestyle. We must make sure to be in the first group, not the second.

Our obligation, as seekers of truth, is to do as Paul writes in Philippians 3:17—"join in follow-ing my example, and observe those who walk according to the pattern you have in us." Paul left no question as to whose will he pursued. His compulsion to preach "the whole purpose of God" (Acts 20:27) made him friends of good people such as Barnabas, Timothy, Aquila and Priscilla. It also made him enemies of false brethren such as Hymenaeus and Philetus (2 Timothy 2:16-18). Will we imitate the selfless, giving pattern of behavior exemplified by Paul, who himself was imitating Christ (1 Corinthians 11:1)? Or will we imitate those who "entice by fleshly desires, by sensuality, those who barely escape from the ones who live in error" (2 Peter 2:18)? It would be tragic to reject the world for Jesus, only to be led astray again by people in the church who are just as worldly.

A Story From The Congregation

Sometimes you just get a good feeling about a church. The people are friendly, the elders are supportive, the worship is enthusiastic, it just seems like a good fit. When a preacher is looking for a place to preach, that's the feeling he and his family want to get.

Peter had that feeling with one church. It was "time to make a change," as the saying goes. And this congregation had expressed a desire for Peter and his family to relocate to help them in the work there. Peter was very much inclined to accept an offer, and he said as much to Henry, one of the church's overseers, over the phone.

Then came "the marriage conversation." The previous preacher, it seemed, had preached rather obsessively with regard to marriage, divorce and remarriage. He held the position that the marriage covenant described in Matthew 19:3-9 applies to all of mankind, regardless of whether a relationship with Jesus exists at the time of the marriage. Henry disagreed, taking the view that those in the world are not bound by this covenant—and therefore a marriage that would not fit the description of Matthew 19 but that was begun when the husband and wife were not Christians could be "grandfathered" in, as it were.

Peter agreed with the other preacher. And he had some discussion with Henry on the subject. He referred to the adulterous marriage of Herod and Herodias that was outside of a covenant with God and yet condemned by John the Baptist (Matthew 14:3-4). He referred to the universal and timeless principles from Genesis 2:24 that Jesus cited in Matthew 19. He pointed out the mandate given for Christians to remain married to non-believers in 1 Corinthians 7:12 and 1 Peter 3:1.

Henry wasn't convinced. But, he insisted, the issue did not touch any of the members there. It was entirely hypothetical. He had no ill will against Peter; he didn't feel that Peter's position on the subject made him any less suited for the work there, and he and the other elders definitely wanted him to come. But he said the subject had been more than adequately covered in recent months, that the position Peter held had been well defended, and that they would like to have Peter's assurance that the "dead horse" would not receive further beatings under his watch.

What Did Peter Tell Henry?

☐ If there is no indication that there are unscriptural marriages in the church, I would be willing to let the issue go—for now. But I have to teach the truth as I understand it if and when the situation calls for it.

☐ I have too much respect for local elders to put myself in a position where I will be in conflict with them on a point of doctrine at some point in the future. And be assured, the "hypothetical" situation won't stay that way forever. You'll need to find a different preacher. God bless.

☐ Love for the truth compels me to not only turn down the position but also to put the word out to other preachers that the congregation there is shaky on this subject. I would hate for some other preacher, even one I don't know, to stumble into the situation I very nearly stumbled into.

A Story From The Bible

You qualify as one of the all-time great Bible villains, I suppose, if the Holy Spirit names a false doctrine after you. Such is the case with Balaam in Revelation 2:14, "who kept teaching Balak to put a stumbling block before the sons of Israel." As sad as that is to say, it is made even worse when we consider that Balaam entered the Bible story as a faithful prophet of the true God. Numbers 22-24 tells the story of how Balak, king of Moab, sought to get Balaam to curse the Israelites, who posed an apparent threat to him and his kingdom as they surged out of Egyptian territory toward the land of Canaan. Most of us know the story of how Balaam insisted that he knew from God Himself that Israel was destined for success, not failure. But also we remember how Balaam kept asking God for a second opinion, as it were—and how his willingness to give God a chance to change His mind seemed to increase every time Balak's promise of reward grew larger. Eventually, a donkey had to teach Balaam a lesson on how to avoid the wrath of God.

Unfortunately for Israel, Balaam persisted in his quest for Balak's treasure. Although Numbers 25 does not say so specifically, the message of Revelation 2:14 indicates clearly that the widespread fornication with Moabite women was Balaam's idea. It would seem he gave up on getting God to curse Israel simply because he asked him to, and realized he could introduce sin into the camp of Israel and accomplish the same goal. The people fell out of favor with God, and God halted their progression until the sin was removed from the camp.

When the church in Pergamum is chastened for tolerating some who held "the teaching of Balaam," it seems to indicate that members there were willing to pursue carnal, selfish goals by introducing sin into the body of Christ; "things sacrificed to idols" and "acts of immorality" are mentioned particularly. Exactly how such behavior in the church would have benefitted the latter day "Balaams" is unclear. What is perfectly clear, however, is God's condemnation of those who would corrupt the local fellowship of saints or tolerate those who do.

Balaam lives even today. As much as has ever been the case, Christians are trying to rationalize all sorts of sinful behavior into the body of Christ. Ironically, this is typically done in the name of "keeping up with the times" or "making the church relevant for the modern day." In truth, pointing the church toward immorality is as old as the church itself. There's nothing "modern" about it.

The end of the Balaam story is tragic. Joshua 13:22 tells us Balaam was killed fighting against the people of God. How could he get to the point where he opposed the very people he blessed? How could he stand violently opposed to a cause God Himself said would succeed? It is difficult to say, other than this is the way the workings of evil progress.

Today, people who follow the pattern of Balaam, preferring selfish goals to righteous ones, will suffer the same condemnation. Those who try to straddle the fence between God and the world invariably wind up falling off on the wrong side, and destroying themselves in the process. The real "donkeys" are the ones who stubbornly hold onto their vices against constant admonitions from the Scriptures and from concerned brethren.

1. What are some examples of things the church generally would have labeled as sin a generation or two ago but are widely accepted today? Is this a good development or a bad one? _____
_____
_____
_____

2. Are there any lessons of history that, if learned, can help us identify patterns of behavior that will take us away from the pattern of Jesus Christ? If so, list them and explain the lesson(s) we should learn. _____

_____

_____

What Did Peter Tell Henry?

☐ If there is no indication that there are unscriptural marriages in the church, I would be willing to let the issue go—for now. But I have to teach the truth as I understand it if and when the situation calls for it.

☑ **I have too much respect for local elders to put myself in a position where I will be in conflict with them on a point of doctrine at some point in the future. And be assured, the "hypothetical" situation won't stay hypothetical forever. You'll need to find a different preacher. God bless.**

☐ Love for the truth compels me to not only turn down the position but also to put the word out to other preachers that the church there is shaky on this subject. I would hate for some other preacher, even one I don't know, to stumble into the situation I very nearly stumbled into.

I'm not a big fan of brotherhood blackballing. I trust my brethren, including my preaching brethren, to use good judgment in their stand for the truth. I don't assume the way I exercise judgment is the only proper way, and I don't criticize others for disagreeing with me; I especially don't criticize them in public. And one elder not being persuaded of the truth, as I see the truth, is hardly the same thing as a congregation supporting error.

Moving to a congregation means submitting to local oversight. That creates a problem for preachers when elders take a stance that, while perhaps not directly countenancing sin, does not promote truth as simply and consistently as possible. I would rather not be in a position where I have to choose between the dictates of an eldership and those of my conscience; when I have a choice, I will avoid that position.

Lesson 11

The Wrong Kind Of Support

Choosing A Spouse Over The Lord

Unconditional love. Unconditional support. Unconditional loyalty. We use phrases such as these to describe the connection between husband and wife. And I suppose some people mean them absolutely. When I use them, though, I trust that it is understood that a commitment to Jesus Christ must always come first. That's one condition that must always apply, whether it is overtly stated or not.

Jesus does not leave this choice up to us. He stated in Luke 14:26, "If anyone comes to Me, and does not hate his own father and mother and wife and children and brothers and sisters, yes, and even his own life, he cannot be My disciple." The New American Standard Bible includes a footnote for the word "hate," suggesting it means, "by comparison of his love for Me." The love for Christ must make all other affections pale in insignificance.

Unfortunately, husbands and wives are sometimes placed in a position where they must choose between supporting their spouse and supporting the Lord. As is the case with all trials, we find in that day of decision where our strongest commitment truly lies. An unwillingness to stand with Him on that day is not just an indication of the depth of our trials; it shows the shallowness of our faith.

A Story From The Office

The economic downturn hit lots of families at church, but perhaps Alex and Sabrina more than most. The pressure from his supervisors ratcheted up exponentially for Alex and the other managers on his sales force: produce results, or else. A twenty-year career, a highly successful one, suddenly looked more precarious than he could have imagined. Sabrina considered going back to work as a precaution, but Alex discouraged it. She had always been at home with the boys, and they wanted to keep it that way if at all possible. And as long as Alex continued to produce on the job, there was no problem.

But after a few months, Alex was showing up less and less at social functions. He

Alex and Sabrina
- Ages: He's 45, she's 41
- Married: 15 years
- Occupations: He's a sales manager, she's a housewife
- Children: Three sons: 12 year old Bryce, 10 year old Garrett, and 6 year old Tyler
Problem: Pressures at work

started missing Wednesday evening Bible study. "Long hours at the office," Sabrina said with a rueful expression whenever someone would ask. She wasn't happy about it, clearly. But then again, she knew Alex was doing what he needed to do to support the family.

Then Sabrina began to pull away a bit as well. Wendy dropped in for a visit one day to make sure all was well and catch up, and Sabrina was glad to see her—until Wendy spotted the travel brochure for a Las Vegas casino on the end table. Suddenly Sabrina got very defensive and evasive. After a bit of prodding, Sabrina admitted that she and Alex were going to Vegas on a company outing in a few weeks.

"It's important for his work that he come and support his team," she insisted. "And wives are expected to be there. We don't really have a choice. And it's not like we are going to go lose a thousand dollars at the blackjack tables."

Peter got Alex to agree to get together for lunch the next Sunday. Claire talked with the boys at the next table while Peter and Wendy poked and prodded. As they had feared, Alex's work had pressured him into participating in several functions that had involved "social drinking." "And that's exactly what it is," Alex said. "Social. I'll nurse one glass of wine the entire evening. And I know all the arguments. But the Bible says don't get drunk, and I don't get drunk."

"But the others at the party do."

"Some of them, sure. I can't help that."

"And what about your influence?" Wendy asked.

"I think he's being a good influence," Sabrina answered. "He's showing them how to be responsible, and he's sober enough where he can be a safe driver if someone needs a ride home."

"And what about the Vegas trip?" I asked. "Are you going to gamble?"

"I might play a hand or two of blackjack, just to fit in," Alex responded. "I've already told Sabrina, I am only going to take a hundred dollars or so with me, and I'll quit if I run out, no matter what."

"Tell the truth," Wendy asked Sabrina privately as they waited for the men to bring the cars around. "Do you really buy into what Alex is saying?"

"I don't know," Sabrina said, with a tear in her eye. "All I know is, he's my husband. He takes care of us, so I am going to take care of him."

My unvoiced concern: The compromising had just begun; precedents were being set that would pave the way for them to abandon their faith entirely.

What Did Wendy Tell Sabrina?

☐ You know how I feel about these things. Make your own mind up. But if you are determined to go down this path, keep it to yourselves. The more this gets out, the more of a problem it will be with the church.

☐ The problem isn't the behavior itself; it's the attitude behind it. Even if you could prove that the occasional drink or $5 bet were permissible (and I'm not at all sure you can), you are doing it because success in business has become more important than your faith.

☐ Drinking is a sin. Gambling is a sin. Choosing sinful companions is a sin. You are enabling each other while you are enabling your companions by rationalizing your choices.

A Story From The Bible

Sapphira was given a choice. Stand for truth, or lie with her husband. She may or may not have appreciated the significance of that decision. She may or may not have anticipated the consequences for choosing poorly. The only thing that really mattered is the choice itself. And she chose her husband.

Acts 5:1-11 relates the story of Sapphira and her husband, Ananias. We are told Ananias decided to donate some of the proceeds from a land sale to the cause of needy saints, but to lie about the details. Sapphira may or may not have agreed with the decision, but she was aware of it and, when push came to shove, supported it.

Of course, when Peter confronted Sapphira with the lie, she had no idea of the price her husband had already paid. Surely she would have confessed to the deception had she known that it had already cost her husband his life. But, unaided by that information, she simply answered from her heart. And her heart was more with her husband than it was with the truth. As a result, she too was struck dead as an example to the early church.

Far from being the source of terror and discouragement that we might have expected, the "great fear" that came upon the church and the entire Jewish community seems to have increased the power of the gospel. Acts 5:14 reads, regarding that time in the history of the church, "And all the more believers in the Lord, multitudes of men and women, were constantly added to their number." Perhaps that should not be seen in the immediate context of the Ananias and Sapphira story; still, there is no reason to believe the incident had any serious ill effects on the morale of those Christians or their effectiveness in bringing their neighbors to a saving faith in Jesus.

Standing for the truth will never discourage seekers of the truth. All big commitments in life will come at a cost; everyone realizes that and anticipates it. Insisting that a connection to Jesus must come before any other connection, even one with a husband or wife, is a difficult argument to make. But the one who truly values a relationship with Jesus will at least give Him a fair hearing.

1. Is saying, "It violates my conscience," always an acceptable rationale for a wife's refusal to accept her husband's authority? Explain and provide examples. _____
_____
_____
_____

2. What are some other situations in which a wife (or husband) might be tempted to use marriage as a rationalization for doing something that ordinarily would be considered sinful. _____
_____
_____
_____

What Did Wendy Tell Sabrina?

☐ You know how I feel about these things. Make your own mind up. But if you are determined to go down this path, keep it to yourselves. The more this gets out, the more of a problem it will be with the church.

☑ **The problem isn't the behavior itself; it's the attitude behind it. Even if you could prove that the occasional drink or $5 bet were permissible (and I'm not at all sure you can), you are doing it because success in business has become more important than your faith.**

☐ Drinking is a sin. Gambling is a sin. Choosing sinful companions is a sin. You are enabling each other while you are enabling your companions by rationalizing your choices.

Personally, I feel the case I make against the occasional drink and the occasional bet is compelling. You may or may not agree. In any case, the undeniable truth is that the values rooted in Jesus that had long characterized Alex were being replaced by values rooted in the world. And by participating with him, Sabrina was enabling him. Pounding away with generalities about "sin" that she was not prepared to accept would only detract from the bigger issue—that of an increasingly worldly approach to life.

The line between passive resistance and passive support can be nebulous. But if Sabrina was to answer to Jesus first and her husband second, she had to find a way to respectfully refuse to participate in actions she felt were sinful. (Needless to say, a conversation with Alex is in order as well.)

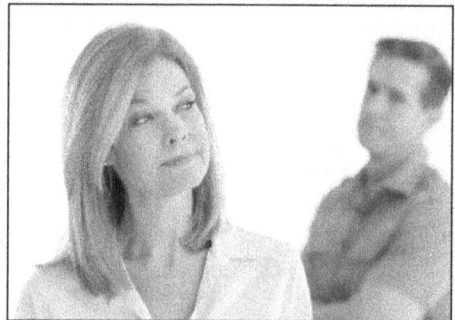

Lesson 11a

When We Don't Agree

The Limitations Of Spiritual Fellowship

What do we mean when we say, "Speak where the Bible speaks"? Simply put, the Bible is God's form of communication with mankind. It takes many forms—history, poetry, legalese, case studies, etc. When God shares His will with us, regardless of form, it is our obligation to accept it as truth and apply it in our lives. We know this from a wide variety of texts. "Sanctify them in the truth; Your word is truth," (John 17:17). "For I am not ashamed of the gospel, for it is the power of God for salvation to everyone who believes, to the Jew first and also to the Greek," (Romans 1:16). "So faith comes from hearing, and hearing by the word of Christ," (Romans 10:17). "In pointing out these things to the brethren, you will be a good servant of Christ Jesus, constantly nourished on the words of the faith and of the sound doctrine which you have been following," (1 Timothy 4:6). With all this in mind, we must require Biblical authority for the things that we do as His servants and that we impose on others. "Whatever you do in word or deed, do all in the name of the Lord Jesus, giving thanks through Him to God the Father," (Colossians 3:17).

The flipside of this argument must be respected as well. We cannot speak "as one who is speaking the utterances of God" (1 Peter 4:11) if there are no such utterances. We may, and should, have strong judgments as to how to carry out His will in our lives; but if those judgments are fundamentally no more than our best effort at understanding His mandates, and not mandates themselves, we have to find a way to live in peace. Being "right" or "wrong" is important, of course, but it is not the only consideration. The matter of meat sacrificed to idols was in the realm of revealed truth for the Romans; if it had not been before, certainly it was when they received Paul's letter, in which he wrote, "nothing is unclean in itself" (Romans 14:14). Binding a command to abstain from such food would reject inspired teaching on the matter. On the other hand, as was the case in Rome, Christians often avoid certain actions for reasons of conscience, not faith. Such matters of indifference can actually become a stumbling block to a weaker brother (Romans 14:13). In such cases we continue to study, and hopefully come to "the unity of the Spirit" (Ephesians 4:3) eventually. But while we wait for that time, Paul says, "Now accept the one who is weak in faith, but not for the purpose of passing judgment on his opinions" (Romans 14:1).

Paul says in the middle of this context, "But you, why do you judge your brother? Or you again, why do you regard your brother with contempt? For we will all stand before the judgment seat of God," (Romans 14:10). It serves no purpose for us eternally to be "right" on a point of doctrine but hold it in the "wrong" way, with disregard for our brethren in Christ. We need to let God do His job of judging, and content ourselves with doing the best we can at submitting.

A Story From The Congregation

"So what exactly is 'the Gospel'?" Stone asked. Peter would have seen trouble in that question even if it hadn't been Stone asking it. And since it was Stone, who had a long history of bringing up argumentative questions just for the sake of being argumentative, Peter figured they were in for a lively exchange. He was right.

Knowing Stone was only asking the question to answer it himself, Peter let him. "It seems to me that Paul defines the gospel in 1 Corinthians 15:3-11 as the death, burial and resurrection of Jesus. Would you agree with that?"

"Well, that depends," Peter said. "If you want to say that is the core of the gospel, that everything derives from that, I would agree. But clearly the gospel is something not just to believe, but also to obey. Romans 10:16 and 2 Thessalonians 1:8 are examples. You can't 'obey' the death, burial and resurrection of Jesus."

"Well, obviously. Still, it shows that there are principles that are more central to the gospel message than other principles. The seven unities of Ephesians 4:4-6, for instance."

"You going somewhere with this, Stone?"

"I'm just saying we can get pretty caught up in the minutia of doctrine to the point where we miss the big picture. If we can come to an agreement on the basics of the gospel, don't you think we ought to pretty much leave the rest of it alone?"

What Did Peter Tell Stone?

☐ We are supposed to be one in doctrine. And the whole gospel is doctrine, not just the parts you think are important. If we can't all speak the same thing, we can't be brethren.

☐ Agreeing on central principles may be all that is "required" of us, but that doesn't mean we can't do better. We should always be trying to find common ground in Jesus. The more, the better.

☐ Deciding what parts of the gospel are "central" is a dangerous precedent. We should be striving together to find the truth of God's word—all of it—and helping one another in its pursuit. Picking and choosing "central" issues for ourselves can quickly become factious.

A Story From The Bible

Say you are a member of a congregation whose members suddenly decided they wanted to be known by a different name. A denominational name, essentially. Or perhaps they quit taking a moral stand against the depravity of society. Maybe they were binding personal judgments as though they were God's law. Or abusing the Lord's Supper? What if the church were rife with jealousy and selfishness? Maybe the church elders didn't actually support such things—but then again, maybe they did. They certainly didn't do anything of substance to stop these corrupting influences.

Would you stand for such things? Or would you take whatever handful of truth-loving souls you might find and start over again, trying to form a fellowship in which God is truly honored and the truth is taught in its fullness?

If you are quick to abandon ship (and perhaps set it on fire on your way) in such circumstances, I encourage you to read 1 Corinthians again. Then reevaluate.

It is difficult to imagine a church that would follow after men (chapters 1-3), tolerate immorality (chapter 5), bind where God has not bound (chapters 8-10), bicker over matters of pride and self-promotion (chapters 12 and 14), and need to have the term "love" redefined for them (chapter 13). How could a church possibly sink so low? How could godly men and women possibly be expected to serve Jesus Christ in such a setting?

But here's another question: Why did Paul not broach the subject of splitting the church?

How many fellowships have you known to divide over issues far less pervasive than the issues in Corinth appear to have been? Such divisions were likely justified as "matters of conscience." But there is little doubt that many if not most of such separations are simply a result of one group of Christians failing to find a way to work with another group of Christians. Often, they failed to find a way because they did not work very hard. Or at all.

Brethren will disagree. Frequently they will disagree over doctrinal matters. No one is suggesting such differences should be swept under the rug. Paul exposed the error and weakness in Corinth and demanded they comply with apostolic authority; in fact, "threatened" would not be too strong a word to describe his warning in 2 Corinthians 13:1-3.

I am not suggesting truth-loving brethren need to "stick it out" under all circumstances. For better or worse, many Christians live in circumstances where alternatives exist, where the option is available to attach themselves to local works that serve God more perfectly. And one certainly could make the case of conscience—that local leadership is forcing all members, including those who disagree, to countenance incorrect or incomplete doctrine, and that such is ample cause for separation. But I am suggesting there is no Bible precedent for voluntarily cutting oneself off from a local fellowship, either for personal reasons or doctrinal reasons. None whatsoever. As people who claim to desire "book, chapter and verse" for their actions, we should consider that before taking a hammer and chisel to the temple of God (1 Corinthians 3:17).

If love truly "bears all things, believes all things, hopes all things, endures all things" (1 Corinthians 13:7), surely brethren will go the extra mile to find enough common ground in Jesus to persevere in fellowship. As long as Bibles and hearts remain open, the possibility remains for "the unity of the Spirit in the bond of peace" (Ephesians 4:2).

1. Who is to determine what issues are worth fighting over, and what issues are worth leaving alone? _____
_____
_____

2. At what point, if ever, does an entire congregation cease to be acceptable to God? Explain your answer, citing Scripture if possible, and the implications of that for the members of that congregation. _____

_____

_____

What Did Peter Tell Stone?

☐ We are supposed to be one in doctrine. And the whole gospel is doctrine, not just the parts you think are important. If we can't all speak the same thing, we can't be brethren.

☐ Agreeing on central principles may be all that is "required" of us, but that doesn't mean we can't do better. We should always be trying to find common ground in Jesus. The more, the better.

☑ **Deciding what parts of the gospel are "central" is a dangerous precedent. We should be striving together to find the truth of God's word—all of it—and helping one another in its pursuit. Picking and choosing "central" issues for ourselves can quickly become factious.**

Striving for unity should know no boundaries—"major" issues, "minor" issues, everything in between. If it's in the Bible, it's truth. God wouldn't have given it to us if He didn't want us to understand it. But that does not mean we pick fights and quarrel over every nuance of doctrine. We search for the truth, certainly—but we do it in a spirit of love, "with great patience and instruction" (2 Timothy 4:2). I am willing to work with anyone who holds to basic Biblical morality (1 Corinthians 6:9-10), accepts the Bible as the standard of divine truth (2 Timothy 3:16-17), and is willing to dwell peaceably in the body of Christ (Titus 3:10-11).

Jesus Himself defined certain principles as "weightier matters" (Matthew 23:23). But that does not mean we will only be judged by those specific things. It is my obligation to pursue "the whole purpose of God" (Acts 20:27) and encourage my brethren to do the same.

Lesson 12

Preparing The Next Generation

Partnership In The Rearing Of Children

It is mandatory that husbands and wives be united in their war against the children. People think this is a joke when they hear this. It is not.

It is not a brutal, bloody war—hopefully not. But it is a war—a war of words, of ideologies, and of priorities. It is a war for supremacy, with battlefields ranging from breakfast menus to homework schedules to extracurricular activities.

No offense intended to any reader not yet old enough to appreciate this, but—no matter what you may pick up from your favorite sitcom—parents are a lot smarter than children. For every ounce of cynicism they have picked up over the years, they have acquired ten pounds of wisdom, education, experience, common sense, and life skills. Children, given their way, will always choose dessert over vegetables, television over chores, sick days over school days. In pursuit of their own way, they will destroy themselves. It is the parents' job to make sure that does not happen.

Parents do not always agree. Parents do not always get along. And children, despite their basic inability to set an alarm or use a napkin, are excellent at exploiting adverse circumstances for their own benefit. A desire to "win" an argument with her husband may move a wife to recruit their child over to "her side." The husband, noticing this effort, may counter with his own. Suddenly the child is in charge of the family. And when decisions are being made solely on the basis of the child's short-term interest (and that's the only kind of interest they have), bad things happen. The animals are now running the zoo. Nothing good can come of that, either for children or for parents.

The child is not to blame in such circumstances. The parents are. They must find a way to interact with respect, disagree privately, support each other publicly, and avoid using the child as a prize to be won, an ally to be recruited, or a friend in whom to confide.

A Story From The Office

Living in a hub for a major airline helped Isaiah spend some quality time at home with his family. But his schedule kept him

Isaiah and Rachelle
- Ages: He's 34, she's 34
- Married: 8 years
- Occupations: He's a airline pilot and military rservist, she's a dental hygienist
- Children: Two 6 year old daughters, Jillian and Eva

Problem: Child-rearing philosophies

away from home more often than not. Rachelle, who went back to work after their girls started school, was left to fill both parenting roles for much of the time. And Jillian and Eva, though adorable, could be a handful. Apiece.

One Sunday there appeared to be some tension. Wendy told Peter the girls were unusually quiet during Bible class. The family ducked out of services quickly without speaking to anyone—very unusual for them. Wendy caught up with Rachelle on Wednesday (Isaiah had a flight) and invited her out for a couples outing when Isaiah returned. That Friday, with the twins at home playing American Girls with Claire, the four grown-ups went out for Mexican food. Afterward they took a walk in the park downtown and talked more privately.

Wendy's instincts proved to be accurate. Rachelle had left the girls with Isaiah instead of at daycare on the previous Friday, a rare weekday at home for him. She returned to find he had spanked Jillian twice—once for refusing to clean her room, once for giving him "attitude" about it afterward. They had quarreled about it the rest of the night, and a good part of Saturday as well.

"It's not that I'm opposed to spanking," Rachelle said. "I have spanked the girls before. But not for something as little as that. Jilly told me that she had cleaned the room, just not as good as he wanted it."

"And you took her word over mine. That's the biggest thing. You need to support me and trust me. You weren't there."

"I can't believe you just said that! 'You weren't there'? You're never there! I run the house completely on my own three weeks out of the month, and then you come in and make up entirely new rules on the spot without my input! How am I supposed to respond to that?"

Unspoken concerns: Rachelle resented being abandoned to be the equivalent of a single parent; Isaiah was "overparenting" to make up for his time away and doing more harm than good.

What Did Peter And Wendy Tell Isaiah And Rachelle?

☐ Isaiah, the fact is, you are not around very much. You are the head of the house, granted. But Rachelle is in better position to decide what's best for the girls on a day-to-day basis.

☐ Rachelle, it's not your job to find out if your husband has a point. It's your job to back him up. The emotional damage a child might receive from getting one spanking too many is nothing compared to what comes from seeing her parents at odds with one another.

☐ Spanking only works if you have a policy and stick to it, both of you. That helps the children see you acting out of a spirit of correction and not just the emotion of the moment. Isaiah, since you are away so much, waiting until Rachelle gets home might be a good idea.

A Story From The Bible

It is difficult for us in the modern day to appreciate the family dynamics of Near Eastern societies four millennia removed from us. But clearly, the family birthright was a sacred and valued tradition—at least, in Abraham's family. The birthright was largely irrelevant for his sons; Isaac was the only legitimate heir and received virtually all of Abraham's inheritance, although gifts were given to Ishmael and Abraham's other sons (Genesis 25:6). But Isaac had twin boys; tradition held that one, generally the elder, would receive a double portion of his father's estate.

Beyond mere physical blessings, though, Isaac passed on spiritual blessings. As the promises made to Abraham were reiterated to Isaac (Genesis 26:24), so also he would pass them on by inspiration to his son. These promises included a land promise, the land of Canaan in which they sojourned; a nation promise, that would be fulfilled in a great nation to live in that land; and a seed promise, which would bless all nations (Genesis 12:1-3; 15:1, 18-20; 17:1-8; 22:15-18).

But which child would receive the birthright? Which would receive the blessing, and with it the spiritual headship of the family? Rebekah was told, in answer to prayer (a rare instance of the Lord speaking to a woman instead of her husband), that it would be the younger child who would dominate (Genesis 25:23). This message, which we must assume she shared with Isaac, clearly pointed to Jacob as the child of promise. Jacob's birth story even illustrates this prophecy: Jacob was born holding onto his older brother Esau's heel, as though he were trying to pull Esau back into the womb so that he could be born first—earning him his name, which translates as, "Supplanter."

Yet for some reason, Isaac was determined to bless Esau instead. Both boys knew Esau was aligned to receive the birthright; why else bargain over it (Genesis 25:27-34)? And Genesis 27 relates how it was only through the intervention of Rebekah and Jacob that Isaac's inspired prophecy of success and dominance landed on the right head. (Isaac's secondary blessing of Jacob in Genesis 28:3-4 may indicate Isaac realized after the fact that he had wronged Jacob.)

Isaac valued Esau's skills in hunting and cooking—an odd values system for a man of faith such as Isaac. Rebekah preferred Jacob—perhaps because he was a "peaceful" man, perhaps because she esteemed the prophecy. But whether the favoritism was based on weighty considerations or shallow ones, clearly the family dynamic became toxic; Jacob was forced to flee for his life and appears never to have seen his mother again, although Genesis 35:27 records a brief meeting many years later with Isaac.

Traditionally Jacob, the deceiver, has been given much of the blame for the disintegration of the family. Esau, called by inspiration an example of an "immoral or godless person" (Hebrews 12:26) who "despised his birthright" (Genesis 25:34) certainly deserves his share. But the problem began with two parents who could not agree on a values system for the rearing of the children.

1. Is it right for a wife to reject her husband's wishes in pursuit of the "greater good" for their child? Explain why or why not. _____
_____
_____

2. What should be the values we celebrate in our children? How might our actions interfere with the pursuit of those values? _____
_____
_____

What Did Peter And Wendy Tell Isaiah And Rachelle?

☐ Isaiah, the fact is, you are not around very much. You are the head of the house, granted. But Rachelle is in better position to decide what's best for the girls on a day-to-day basis.

☑ **Rachelle, it's not your job to find out if your husband has a point. It's your job to back him up. The emotional damage a child might receive from getting one spanking too many is nothing compared to what comes from seeing her parents at odds with one another.**

☑ **Spanking only works if you have a policy and stick to it, both of you. That helps the children see you acting out of a spirit of correction and not just the emotion of the moment. Isaiah, since you are away so much, waiting until Rachelle gets home might be a good idea.**

I would never suggest a husband cede his authority in any area of the family—although in this instance, Isaiah might want to think about it. Certainly he should be in communication with his wife about situations that may be contributing in the short term to behavior that he might consider rebellious, and then take that information into account when making a discipline decision.

The main thing is that husband and wife act as one. Set rules, and only deviate from them by mutual agreement. Don't be afraid to wait to act; trust and value your spouse's judgment. Never, ever, allow the children to see their parents at odds with one another. The stability of their home should be the one absolute, unquestioned constant in their lives.

Lesson 12a

The Future Of The Church

Develping A New Generation Of Leaders

"Our young people are the future of the church." I've heard brethren say that a hundred times if I've heard it once. I usually try to chime in and suggest that they are a tremendously important part of our present as well. But I understand the point. The elders, deacons, preachers, and wives of all of the above will largely if not mostly come from the crop of children and young adults we have now.

But what does that mean for us today? Do we imagine that they will learn how to serve effectively in those roles simply by being among godly men and women for a few hours a week? Or is there more we can do?

We all know Proverbs 22:4—"Train up a child in the way he should go, even when he is old he will not depart from it." The adage is true as much now as ever; if you're failing to plan, you're planning to fail. Future success comes from current planning. That has its roots in the home, of course; parents train their children to love the Lord, respect authority, show appreciation, worship heartily and prioritize. Children can certainly grow up to serve God apart from supportive parents, and supportive parents are by no means a guarantee of future success. ("Proverbs" are, by their nature, generalizations; there are plenty of exceptions.) But we certainly ought to utilize the best asset we have.

Beyond that, the church can help itself by helping its young people. Opportunities to acquire and practice important "adult" skills (teaching, leading worship, showing hospitality, etc.) should be provided, and unconditional support along with them; unless they try to lead "Stairway to Heaven" as a worship song or something equally objectionable, shower them with praise. And even when it is necessary to explain "the way of God more accurately" (Acts 18:26), do it privately and with oceans of kindness.

Done well, these young people will grow to be able to offer these lessons to the next generation—and do it even better than we did it for them.

A Story From The Congregation

Lots of college students from out of town try to be as invisible as possible in their new church surroundings—leave town most weekends, miss most mid-week Bible studies, rarely participate. Trent was the exact opposite. He told the elders his first weekend in town that he wanted to be considered a member of the congregation in every sense of the word, and that he wanted to be put to work. So he led singing (perhaps not quite as well as he thought he did, but still pretty well), offered several invitations on Wednesday evenings, even volunteered to teach the junior high class. He was a real asset.

After a couple of years, though, it was obvious that he was getting frustrated with the group, and especially with the elders. He had a meeting or two with the elders, and since his demeanor wasn't getting any better, Peter assumed they had not gone as Trent had hoped. Peter even thought he heard a heavy sigh coming from one of the elders one time when Trent came in the building. There had not been anything resembling an incident; Trent was not that type. Still, it was starting to get awkward.

After a sermon entitled, "Taking the Initiative," Trent made a point of approaching Peter in the parking lot. They stood there and talked for about fifteen minutes.

"Do you really think people will do that? Take the initiative, I mean?" he asked earnestly. "Because I'm getting pretty frustrated myself at the indifference and laziness I see in some of the members here."

"Don't you think that's a bit harsh?"

"I don't think so. It really seems like we're just keeping house here. There are lost souls out there."

"Don't I know it."

"But what are we doing about it? I approached the elders awhile back about doing a concentrated weekend of studies focused directly on bringing souls to Christ. Not interested. Then a month ago I suggested a training class for how to talk to your neighbors about Jesus. Not interested."

"Did they give you a reason?"

"They didn't have to. They're scared. Scared of new people, scared of new ideas, scared of growing too fast. They'd rather keep things the way they are than change things and maybe get better."

What Did Peter Tell Trent?

☐ Personally, I think your ideas are terrific. I'll talk to the elders and get them on board. Thanks for your zeal and your love for the Lord.

☐ The job of elder involves a lot of moving parts. Decisions that look simple on our end may not be quite as simple on theirs. You just have to have confidence that they are godly men being led by the Gospel. Be patient, and don't grow weary in well-doing.

☐ I appreciate your enthusiasm. But you may be getting into a dangerous area. It's our job to submit to the elders. Telling them how to do their job is not submitting. Maybe you would do well to hold off on the "new ideas" for a while.

A Story From The Bible

How could it be that a young man (probably a teenager) could be emotionally and, more importantly, spiritually prepared to travel the world preaching the gospel against ferocious opposition? It was no accident. His Jewish mother and grandmother trained him well in the Scriptures (2 Timothy 1:5)—evidently without the help of, and perhaps even against the wishes of, his Gentile father who did not even allow Timothy to be circumcised (Acts 16:1-3). His knowledge of sacred things from childhood guided him to "the wisdom that leads to salvation through faith which is in Christ Jesus" (2 Timothy 3:14-15).

Largely because of the good groundwork that had been laid, Paul was able to instruct Timothy in "the standard of sound words which you have heard from me, in the faith and love which are in Christ Jesus" (2 Timothy 1:13). Then, having received Paul's words of instruction, Timothy's task was to "entrust these to faithful men who will be able to teach others also" (2 Timothy 2:2). In this way, repeated generations can benefit from the initial truth that was "once for all handed down to the saints" (Jude 3).

Perhaps the most important part of the process for Timothy was the appointment of congregational overseers. Timothy and Titus, another young protégé of Paul, were to "appoint elders in every city" (Titus 1:5). These men were to assume the oversight of their respective local congregations, under the authority of Jesus, the Chief Shepherd (1 Peter 5:1-4). These men, guided by the words of inspiration given by Timothy and others, would be in position to help the group collectively glorify God, protect the flock from internal and external threats, and to preserve the tradition of submission to apostolic authority for another generation.

We also read in 1 Timothy 3 of the appointment of deacons—special servants of the church under the oversight of the elders. Little specific is said of their tasks. But in the context of 1 Timothy, it is clear that a primary focus if not the primary focus of deacons should be to prepare themselves to be elders. If men are to be tested before being approved as deacons (1 Timothy 3:10), then it is reasonable to see service as deacon as being preparatory for greater service. Jesus Himself said, "He who is faithful in a very little thing is faithful also in much" (Luke 16:10). What is true for material possessions is just as true for spiritual stewardship. The more opportunities we give men to serve and succeed in the church, the more confidence the church will have in them (and they will have in themselves) for larger tasks.

1. What can a young man do to prepare to be an elder or a deacon later on in life? ____
   _____
   _____
   _____

2. To what roles should young women aspire? How can older women help them prepare for those roles? Cite Scripture. _____
   _____
   _____
   _____

What Did Peter Tell Trent?

☐ Personally, I think your ideas are terrific. I'll talk to the elders and get them on board. Thanks for your zeal and your love for the Lord.

☑ **The job of elder involves a lot of moving parts. Decisions that look simple on our end may not be quite as simple on theirs. You just have to have confidence that they are godly men being led by the Gospel. Be patient, and don't grow weary in well-doing.**

☐ I appreciate your enthusiasm. But you may be getting into a dangerous area. It's our job to submit to the elders. Telling them how to do their job is not submitting. Maybe you would do well to hold off on the "new ideas" for a while.

This is all about perception. Preachers, and members in general, should always want to be perceived as supporting the elders, and not as being a wet blanket. So approving or disapproving the particular idea is not as big a consideration as promoting a loving and cooperative working arrangement.

If in Peter's spot, I might go to the elders and inquire why they disapproved of an idea I ordinarily would support, but I would not do it in such a way as to encourage dissent. I might caution a young person who is acting "too big for his britches," but not in such a way as to dampen his enthusiasm. We (and by "we," I mean "I") need the energy and vitality that younger Christians bring just as much as younger Christians need the caution and patience that maturity brings.

www.ingramcontent.com/pod-product-compliance
Lightning Source LLC
LaVergne TN
LVHW061328060426
835511LV00012B/1910